Chief Supervisor：徐义雄 Yixiong Xu

Mastermind，Translator，Writer，Painter，Composer，Singer & Recorder：张一平 Shirley Yiping Zhang

Advisors：蒋亚平　 Yaping Jiang

　　　　　史蒂芬·H. 罗宾耐特　 Stephen H. Robinette（USA）

　　　　　满维起　 Weiqi Man

English Directors：麦克·乔伊斯 Mike Joyce（UK）

　　　　　　　　　严文荣·沙芬 Wenrong Yan Schaefer（USA）

Music Directors：蒙伟业 Weiye Meng（Piano Player）　　马　萱 Xuan Ma

Painting Directors：韩学中 Xuezhong Han　　吴　彤 Tong Wu

　　　　　　　　　卢文清 Wenqing Lu　　孙　琪 Qi Sun

　　　　　　　　　李　刚 Gang Li　　陶　辉 Hui Tao

Responsible Editors：

Software Developer：张　全 Charlie Quan Zhang

Sound Engineers：欧建德 Jiande Ou　　张红阳 Hongyang Zhang

Art Designers：周红叶 Tina Hongye Zhou　　罗诗忆 Shiyi Luo　　徐洁斌 Jiebin Xu

Publisher：Jinan University Press

Producers：Shenzhen E-Bridge Science and Technology Development Co. , Ltd.

　　　　　Jiangsu E-Bridge Culture Development Co. , Ltd.

Enjoy and Paint Chinese Paintings

Listen to and Sing Chinese (Poetry) Songs

Read and Recite Chinese Poetry and Vocabulary

Together with Me
LEARN CHINESE CULTURE & LANGUAGE
by Enjoying **Paintings, Music & Poetry**

SHI HUA YUE ZONGHE YISHU HANYU

诗·画·乐：
综合艺术汉语

Mastermind, Translator, Writer, Painter, Composer, Singer & Recorder: 张一平 Shirley Yiping Zhang

Advisors: 蒋亚平 Yaping Jiang

史蒂芬•H.罗宾耐特 Stephen H. Robinette（USA）

满维起 Weiqi Man

English Directors: 麦克•乔伊斯 Mike Joyce（UK）　严文荣•沙芬 Wenrong Yan Schaefer（USA）

Music Directors: 蒙伟业 Weiye Meng（Piano Player）　马萱 Xuan Ma

Painting Directors: 韩学中 Xuezhong Han　吴彤 Tong Wu

卢文清 Wenqing Lu　孙琪 Qi Sun

李刚 Gang Li　陶辉 Hui Tao

暨南大学出版社
JINAN UNIVERSITY PRESS

中国·广州

图书在版编目（CIP）数据

诗·画·乐：综合艺术汉语 = Together with Me：Learn Chinese Culture and Language by Enjoying Paintings，Music and Poetry/张一平著 . —广州：暨南大学出版社，2013.5
ISBN 978 – 7 – 5668 – 0502 – 7

Ⅰ.①诗…　　Ⅱ.①张…　　Ⅲ.①汉语—对外汉语教学—语言读物
Ⅳ.①H195.5

中国版本图书馆 CIP 数据核字（2013）第 045775 号

出版发行：暨南大学出版社

地　　址：	中国广州暨南大学	
电　　话：	总编室（8620）85221601	
	营销部（8620）85225284　85228291　85228292（邮购）	
传　　真：	（8620）85221583（办公室）　　85223774（营销部）	
邮　　编：	510630	
网　　址：	http：//www. jnupress. com　http：//press. jnu. edu. cn	

排　　版：	广州市天河星辰文化发展部照排中心
印　　刷：	佛山市浩文彩色印刷有限公司

开　　本：	890mm×1240mm　1/32
印　　张：	3.625
字　　数：	100 千
版　　次：	2013 年 5 月第 1 版
印　　次：	2013 年 5 月第 1 次

定　　价：68.00 元（附送 DVD – ROM 光盘一张）

Foreword

Hello, nice to meet you. I am Shirley Yiping Zhang, the author of this product. Thank you for choosing this product.

When you pick up this little booklet and the DVD, you have touched a part of *E-Bridge Cross-Culture and Comprehensive Art*, which I have been studying, thinking and exploring since 2000.

Maybe you would like to ask: What is the *E-Bridge Cross-Culture and Comprehensive Art*? Why did I create it? Who are its target users?

The purpose I created this product is to help non-Chinese speakers to learn Chinese culture and language in the process of enjoying Chinese paintings, music and poetry. It can also be used for Chinese teachers or students who are learning Chinese language and culture as an accessible teaching or study resource. If you are one of them, you are welcome.

Currently the *E-Bridge Cross-Culture and Comprehensive Art* includes five main series and some sub-series:

I. Vocal, bilingual Chinese poems, paintings and articles series

II. Stories behind Shirley's Chinese paintings and music series

III. Shirley created music for Chinese classical poems and singing series

VI. Shirley's bilingual Chinese folk songs series

V. Shirley's Chinese paintings series

—Chinese Gongbi Paintings

—Chinese Xieyi Paintings

—Chinese Mixed Gongbi & Xieyi Paintings

—Chinese Mogu Paintings

—Chinese Baimiao Paintings

The product in your hand is mainly made up of the Series I. Vocal, bilingual Chinese poems, paintings and articles series, and a part of the content of the Series III, includes:

1. Chinese Classical Poetry Series

2. Articles on Chinese Culture Series

3. Original Music & Singing Series

4. Chinese Painting Series

It is just the Volume One, and its main content are shown as below.

The Poetry and Article Section consists of:

—Chinese classical poems by some famous poets of the Tang Dynasty (618 A. D. −907 A. D.), the Song Dynasty (960 A. D. − 1279 A. D.) and the Qing Dynasty (1644 A. D. − 1911 A. D.)

In the cultural background part, mainly I have made some brief introductions of the development of Chinese poetry, painting and relationship between poetry and music and so on.

By reading the articles, listening to the records, and following me to read or sing the poems, you would be able to know the meaning of the poems, remember the Chinese characters, and learn their cultural background more easily.

The Music and Singing Part consists of:

—12 pieces of music I created for the Poems

—12 songs of poems I sang in Chinese

—12 songs of poems I sang in English

—12 pieces of piano music played by my music professor

I would like to help you to remember or recite the poems easily by listening to my singing the poems in Chinese; to help you to understand the poems more directly by listening to my singing the poems in English; and to help you to feel the poems with your heart and to recite the poems more naturally by singing the poems by yourself along with the music that I have offered you. I do hope that my idea, practice and exploration will work with you indeed.

The Painting and Calligraphy Part consists of:

—12 Chinese paintings I painted for Chinese classical poems

—12 groups of Chinese calligraphy of the poems

—96 Chinese paintings as the Chinese culture background

I painted the 12 paintings according to the artistic conception of the 12 poems, including the poems inscribed in calligraphy and stamps, to help you to understand the meaning of the poems artistically and directly. Most of the 12 paintings in the core series are my assignments for the Chinese National Academy of Arts at which I have been a graduate student since 2011. I learned to paint them following Mr. Bonian Ren, added my own calligraphy, translation and something more to them.

Since I just used Chinese Xieyi Painting to express the Chinese Poems' meanings, it is just a little part of Chinese painting. It cannot show you the outline of Chinese painting.

By helping you to know more about Chinese paintings, and avoiding misleading you, also, I chose some of my other paintings that I painted as my assignments for CNAA and for China Central Academy of Fine Arts, as the background, to help you to know more about Chinese painting and culture.

I do hope that both you and I will learn something by studying these great poets, artists and their art works together, we are able to smell and enjoy the fragrance of the numerous beautiful flowers in the gardens of Chinese culture, arts and language.

The manifestation mode of the product is music, paintings, poetry and articles, to express the ideas of the work by songs, pictures, recitations and words.

This product is just a beginning of the series. Along with the time, when the Volume Two, Volume Three, and more have been published, you will see a structure of groups of the music, paintings, poetry and articles, to support the series product as the pillars of the cross-culture and comprehensive Chinese art series products.

The content framework of the product is made up of poems and includes:

Songs of Spring

Landscape

Love

Farewell

Philosophy

Encouragement

In future editions, the content list of the series will be enlarged, and then extend to more subfamilies.

The Theoretical Basis of This Product

Art's instrumental character, Chinese paintings' comprehensiveness, Chinese primary words' universality, stability and productiveness, make up the theoretical basis of the product.

In My Opinion

—Art is, in essence, a tool. Artists express their thoughts and feelings in different art languages, governments use the ideas in the arts to help them to manage their countries and ordinary people choose arts to please themselves. Just like the different tableware on a dining table can substitute for, complement and support each other to help the diner to enjoy his food more comfortably, sister arts can also interact to affect the audience more naturally. Combining the process of learning a culture or a language with the process of enjoying other various art forms, will make the whole process more interesting and enjoyable, and help learners to grasp knowledge and skills more easily.

—Traditional Chinese arts are essentially comprehensive. Chinese painting is made up of poetry, calligraphy, painting and stamp; Chinese classical poems were sung in ancient times; Chinese calligraphy and paintings come from the same rootstock; Chinese traditional art theory emphasizes that a good painting should include the artistic conception of a poem and a good poem should include artistic conception of a painting. By enjoying the comprehensive art (including paintings, music, poems and articles) in this product, you will just be learning Chinese culture and language naturally.

—Chinese classical poems are mainly made up of Chinese primary words. Chinese primary words are universal (they are used by all Chinese speakers), stable (they have been using since they were created) and they have prolificacy (they are the roots of new words). Learning Chinese classical poetry is the best way to encounter Chinese primary words and to open the gate of Chinese language and culture. Therefore, almost all Chinese children start their Chinese learning by reciting classical poems.

Based on the above understanding, I choose Chinese painting as one of this product's media, focusing on the core of Chinese paintings-poetry and adding music, languages (Chinese and English), literature (poetry comments), historical background (about the poets and the stories behind the poems), to create a new and unique comprehensive art, to help non-Chinese speakers to know more about Chinese culture and language artistically, easily and naturally.

The Mode of Transmission

It will be delivered with multi-media style, Internet, paper, DVD, TV, mobile phone and face to face.

After my studying, thinking about and exploring on the project for more than 10 years, with the good help of many people and organizations, the first little publication of the series products has been dedicated to you. The subsequent products will be developed and published regularly.

I do hope it will be of some help for you to learn Chinese culture and language. And I would really like to receive your comments, suggestions and get your feedback and good directions.

Participators of This Product

During the process of creating and editing, I have gotten so much care, help and direction from so many people and organizations. I would really like to thank them and introduce them to you with a grateful heart.

Chief Supervisor:

徐义雄先生 Mr. Yixiong Xu (China) —The President of Jinan University Press; it was him who suggested the idea of creating a cross-cultural research project in 2009 and since then, he and his team have been directing, helping and supporting me with my work on it.

Advisors:

蒋亚平教授 Prof. Yaping Jiang (China) —The founder of and the first editor in chief of *People's Daily Online* and Nieman Scholar of Harvard University, Deputy Secretary-general of China Land Science Society and the former President of China's Land Resources Newspaper Office; he led me into the Internet field in 1997 and he has encouraged me and given me good advice about my study, thinking and exploration on the project since 2005.

史蒂芬·H. 罗宾耐特先生 Mr. Stephen H. Robinette (USA) — Assistant Vice President of Missouri State University, he has given me many kind directions, much advice and actual help on this project and American culture study since 2009.

满维起教授 Prof. Weiqi Man (China) —Executive Deputy Dean of Chinese Painting School at Chinese National Academy of Arts, tutor of masters students, a member of the Chinese Artists Association. He has directed me to paint in person and he has encouraged and supported me to study, research and explore this project at CNAA since 2011.

English Directors:

麦克·乔伊斯先生 Mr. Mike Joyce (UK) —A native English speaker, he has been my English tutor since 2002. He has checked all of the articles and text files for this project.

严文荣·沙芬博士 Dr. Wenrong Yan Schaefer (USA) —The Asian Arts and Letters Coordinator in Missouri State University, she has checked the "Foreword" and corrected my writing.

宫小欧先生 Mr. Sean Xiaoou Gong (USA) —My first private tutor and schoolfellow in America, with his great effort and patience and in his vacation and free time, he helped me hold the essential knowledge and skills in the most difficult crosses.

Music Directors:

蒙伟业教授 Prof. Weiye Meng (China) —A music professor who graduated from the Central Conservatory of Music. He checked and corrected my music score, coached me in my singing, directed me in making the recordings and accompanied me on the piano for all the songs on the recording.

马萱老师 Ms. Xuan Ma (China) —My first music teacher from 2002 to 2007. She witnessed how I created more than 130 pieces of music for Chinese poems. She coached me to sing the poems for the project in Beijing in 2012 and she directed a part of my singings and record for this project in Shenzhen in 2012.

Painting Directors：

韩学中教授 Prof. Xuezhong Han （China） —Director of Teaching Department of Graduate School and Chinese Painting School at Chinese National Academy of Arts, a judge of the senior professional titles of CNAA, a member of the Council of the Research Society of Chinese Gongbi Zhong Cai（Painting with Exact Delineation and Enriched Colors）of Chinese Artists Association, he instructed me in the painting colors, structures and in my transition from an amateur painter to be a professional painter.

吴彤老师 Mr. Tong Wu （China） —Deputy Director of Teaching Department of the Chinese Painting School at Chinese National Academy of Arts, he helped and directed me most in my Chinese painting at CNAA.

卢文清老师 Mr. Wenqing Lu （China） —My instructor of Chinese Flower and Bird Painting and my Class Adviser at Chinese National Academy of Arts. He directed me in all my paintings and nature sketches at CNAA.

孙琪老师 Mr. Qi Sun （China） —A member of the Chinese Artists Association, he helped me choose Chinese National Academy of Arts to study and to work on the project, he directed me not only on Chinese Flower and Bird Painting, but also on Chinese Landscapes.

李刚老师 Mr. Gang Li （China） —My first teacher of Landscape at China Central Academy of Fine Arts and my Class Adviser, the good foundation that was made at CAFA helped me become a graduate student and to work on the project continuously.

陶辉教授 Prof. Hui Tao （China） —My first Chinese painting teacher who taught me for 8 years since 2003, and it laid the basic foundations for me to enter the art schools in Beijing and work on the project.

Software Developer：

张全先生 Mr. Charlie Quan Zhang（China）—Assistant General Manager of the network company of Securities Times Newspaper Office and my work partner. He developed the software related to this project.

Art Designers：

周红叶小姐、罗诗忆先生 Ms. Tina Hongye Zhou and Mr. Shiyi Luo（China）—They did the art design of the covers of the book, DVD and the web site.

Responsible Editors and Proof-readers：

I would also like to thank the other professors, tutors and friends for their good help：

江泓博士 Dr. Hong Jiang（China）—He checked a part of art works for the project and he gave me some good directions and encouragements in person.

霍学文博士 Dr. Xuewen Huo（China）—He offered much actual practical help during my most difficult times of working on this project.

马英先生 Mr. Ying Ma（China）—He introduced me to some famous scholars of Chinese culture and improved the quality of the project.

张根记先生 Mr. Genji Zhang（China）—He heard my ideas about this project and gave me some good directions.

方竹兰博士 Dr. Zhulan Fang（China）—A professor and tutor of doctoral students at Renmin University of China, visiting scholar at Stanford University and University of Sussex, she gave me much good advice and practical help.

王华博士 Dr. Hua Wang（China）—The President of Guangdong University of Business Studies , former Vice President of Jinan University and a tutor of doctoral students, he offered the practical help for my first translated series of books and the connection between the publishing house and me.

金凤强先生 Mr. Fengqiang Jin（China）—The Assistant President of Jinan University Press and General Manager of Marketing Company of Jinan University Press, he did many jobs related to the product design and he organized this product's publishing work.

张晓岗老师 Ms. Xiaogang Zhang（China）—A senior English teacher, she has checked all my poem translations and the "Foreword".

Mr. Ben Moore（USA）—He listened to all my English singing and helped to correct my pronunciation.

Mr. James Broadbent（Canada）—He has corrected all my translations of the poems and one article.

Dr. Dennis Hart（USA）—He has corrected some of my poetry translations for the project.

Mr. William Gary（USA）—He has corrected some of my poetry translations for the project. .

Dr. Steve Olson（USA）—He has corrected some of my translations of the poems for the project.

Dr. J. Darragh M. Elliott（Canada）—An art appraiser and singer, he has critiqued my art and he has provided assistance in developing my singing abilities. He has corrected some of my poems.

Dr. Bill R. Booth（USA）—A Professor Emeritus of Arts and my American art mentor, he has given me much good advice since 2009.

周毅然先生 Mr. Yiran Zhou（USA）—A Chinese teacher in America, he has checked a part of my writing and he has given me a hand with this project.

张红阳先生 Mr. Hongyang Zhang（China）—The Music Director of Shenzhen Red Culture Art Spread Co. Ltd. , who offered much convenience for my music job in his company.

欧德建先生 Mr. Dejian Ou（China）—Sound Engineer, he made

the recording and mixed of the music and singing for the project.

徐洁斌先生 Mr. Jiebin Xu (China) —An art designer, he helped me deal with some photos of the product.

田松青先生 Mr. Songqing Tian (China) —Assistant President of Shanghai Ancient Books Publishing House, he gave me much good advice on how to publish this product.

程培松先生 Mr. Peisong Cheng (China) —The Deputy Editor-in-Chief of Shanghai Securities Times Newspaper Office, he gave me much good advice about how to publish this publication.

郑初一先生 Mr. Chuyi Zheng (China) —A Department Director at Shanghai Securities Times Newspaper Office, he offered me actual help on how to publish this publication.

张辉先生 Mr. Hui Zhang (China) —An editor from Beijing Office of Tianjin People's Fine Arts Publishing House, he gave me much good advice.

杨广印同学 Mr. Guangyin Yang (China) —An artist from Shandong, the former monitor of our class at CAFA, he offered much help and advice on the project in CNAA in Beijing.

刘治平同学 Mr. Zhiping Liu (China) —An artist from Liaoning, my former classmate in CAFA, he offered much help and advice on the project in Beijing.

吴德华、曹雪芬老师 Mr. Dehua Wu and Mrs. Xuefen Cao (China) —My former colleagues and they offered much help in Beijing.

于延杰女士 Mrs. Yanjie Yu (China) —My former colleague and she offered much help while I was in Shenzhen.

The tutors who have taught and directed me face to face at Chinese National Academy of Arts：田黎明教授 Prof. Liming Tian，许俊教授 Prof. Jun Xu，张鸿飞教授 Prof. Hongfei Zhang，苗在新教授 Prof. Zaixin Miao，李乃宙教授 Prof. Naizhou Li，何延喆教授 Prof. Yanzhe He，韩敬伟教授 Prof. Jingwei Han，曾先国教授 Prof. Xianguo Zeng,

王同君教授 Prof. Tongjun Wang，林若曦教授 Prof. Ruoxi Lin，刘选让教授 Prof. Xuanrang Liu，刘万鸣副教授 Associate Prof. Wanming Liu，潘樱副教授 Associate Prof. Ying Pan，赵国经、王美芳老师 Mr. Guojing Zhao and Mrs. Meifang Wang，田云鹏先生 Mr. Yunpeng Tian，曹传真先生 Mr. Chuanzhen Cao，吴冰博士 Dr. Bing Wu，刘波博士 Dr. Bo Liu，曹建华博士 Dr. Jianhua Cao，李雪松老师 Mr. Xuesong Li. 唐永力教授 Prof. Yongli Tang，陈平教授 Prof. Ping Chen，李洋教授 Prof. Yang Li，苏百君教授 Prof. Baijun Su，崔晓东教授 Prof. Xiaodong Cui，姚明京教授 Prof. Mingjing Yao，李铁生副教授 Associate Prof. Tiesheng Li，刘庆和副教授 Associate Prof. Qinghe Liu，于光华副教授 Associate Prof. Guanghua Yu，姚舜熙副教授 Associate Prof. Shunxi Yao，刘荣副教授 Associate Prof. Rong Liu，毕建勋副教授 Associate Prof. Jianxun Bi，岳黔山副教授 Associate Prof. Qianshan Yue，丘挺副教授 Associate Prof. Ting Qiu，徐海副教授 Associate Prof. Hai Xu，谢青博士 Dr. Qing Xie，金瑞老师 Mr. Rui Jin，张弓老师 Mr. Gong Zhang，林彬老师 Mr. Bin Lin and 张猛老师 Mr. Meng Zhang.

Especially, I would like to thank my doctors：张秋娟教授 Prof. Qiujuan Zhang，刘郁博士 Dr. Yu Liu，宋阳医生 Dr. Yang Song，刘蓉医生 Dr. Rong Liu，刘映霞博士 Dr. Yingxia Liu，袁志东医生 Dr. Zhidong Yuan，林琦医生 Dr. Qi Lin and many other doctors and nurses for their good help.

I would also like to thank Shenzhen Securities Information Co. Ltd. , Shenzhen City Panorama Co. Ltd. and my bosses：周明先生 Mr. Ming Zhou and 郑颂博士 Dr. Song Zheng for their sincere understanding, help and support.

Shenzhen E-Bridge Science and Technology Development Co. , Ltd. ; Jiangsu E-Bridge Culture Development Co. , Ltd. and Shenzhen Red Culture Art Spread Co. , Ltd. offered the technology and record support.

Mastermind, Translator, Writer, Painter, Composer, Singer and

Recorder of the product: 张一平 Shirley Yiping Zhang (China) —I was born in Beijing. I have majored in Chinese language and literature, world economics, journalism (news), international business administration and business administration, English and Chinese painting at eight universities in China and in USA. Now I am a full-time Chinese painting graduate student at Chinese National Academy of Arts in Beijing.

I started to write about Chinese culture in English in 1999, and I had the idea of starting a cross-cultural project after I heard how much different English in different countries while on a travel to Europe in 2000. Then I masterminded and translated (from English to Chinese) the first E-Bridge series books, *Together with Me: Learn True American English* which includes 4 volumes, 4 CDs and contained 0.93 million words. With good help from a group of American, Canadian and Chinese friends, it was published by Jinan University Press in Oct. , 2002.

I started to learn vocal music in Nov. , 2002, and re-started to learn painting in 2003 (my childhood dream was to be an artist of painting and music, but I stopped painting since I entered university), then I started to create music for Chinese poems, to sing them in Chinese, and to translate the poems, folk songs into English while, at the same time, I founded the web site in 2005.

In 2007, I started to create paintings for Chinese classical poems and I tried singing them in English.

In 2008, I became a part-time student of Beijing Foreign Studies University online, then I went to Missouri State University, USA, as a master degree student even though I had already got a doctoral degree.

From 2009 to 2011, I held 3 art exhibitions, visited 23 public schools, 4 universities, an arts centre and participated in a World Language Conference to introduce Chinese culture by means of my own comprehensive art with painting, singing, poetry and lectures 42 times in USA.

From 2010 until now, I have been a full-time Chinese Painting student at China Central Academy of Fine Arts and at Chinese National Academy of Arts in Beijing.

My dream is to create a unique, artistic series product and service that is focused on Chinese poetry, painting and music, to help non-Chinese speakers learn Chinese culture and language naturally, artistically and more easily; to help Chinese teenagers from the remote and poor areas by inviting them to be this project's learners and participators.

I wish it to be mainly delivered by Internet, multi-media, and face to face.

Now I have made a model. I will invite more professional artists, musicians, scholars of Chinese teenagers to work with me in future editions, to creat more and better works along with the time.

As the initiator of this project, I would really like to hear your comments and suggestions and hope to get your direction and advice.

Thank you for choosing this publication once more.

Sincerely yours,
Shirley Yiping Zhang
May 4, 2013
www. ebridge. cn
shirley@ ebridge. cn

CONTENTS

Foreword

01. 春晓—A Spring Morning

春晓—chūn xiǎo

唐—táng　孟浩然—mèng hào rán

春眠不觉晓—chūn mián bù jué xiǎo，

处处闻啼鸟—chù chù wén tí niǎo。

夜来风雨声—yè lái fēng yǔ shēng，

花落知多少—huā luò zhī duō shǎo。

Chun Xiao —A Spring Morning

By Meng Haoran　Tang Dynasty

Sleeping on a spring night, I've missed the dawn.

Everywhere I hear the songs of birds.

In the night's wind and rain,

How many flowers have fallen?

About the Poet

Meng Haoran 孟浩然 mèng hào rán (689 – 740) was born in Xiangyang, in today's Hubei Province. Apart from spending a short time in the capital—Chang'an City, to pursue his career, and traveling in Wu and Yue in today's Jiangsu and Zhejiang, he lived in the Xiangyang area for most of his life.

Meng Haoran is as famous as Wang Wei, because of their friendship and their prominence as Idyll and Landscape Poets.

Succeeding Tao Yuanming (about 365 – 427) and Xie Lingyun (385 – 433), he and Wang Wei (701 – 761) are regarded as the predecessors of the Idyll and Landscape Poetry in the Tang Dynasty.

The language of his poems is very clear and simple, the feelings are kind and true, and they are unique, free and full of breath of life.

He, therefore, had a great reputation in the Tang Dynasty. He was a good friend of Wang Wei, Li Bai, Wang Changling and Du Fu and he was admired by them.

He and Wang Wei are known as "Wang and Meng" in the history of Chinese poetry.

Enjoy the Poem

Chun Xiao — A Spring Morning is a very simple but quite famous Chinese classical poem by Meng Haoran. In just 4 lines and 20 Chinese characters, it describes a very vivid and fresh glimpse of life.

The first two lines：春眠不觉晓，处处闻啼鸟 chūn mián bù jué xiǎo, chù chù wén tí niǎo—Sleeping on a spring night, I've missed the dawn. Everywhere I hear the songs of birds.

The last two lines：夜来风雨声，花落知多少 yè lái fēng yǔ shēng, huā luò zhī duō shǎo—In the night's wind and rain, how many flowers have fallen?

Catching the first feeling at a split second when the poet woke up on the spring morning, this poem writes about what the poet heard and thought, describing the vibrant scenery of spring morning after raining. Instead of describing it from a visual angle, this poem captures the sounds of spring, from the aural angle, writes about what the poet heard from his room rather than what he saw out of the door. In the simplest language, the poem leads readers into a boundless spring scenery, and creates huge room for readers to imagine what that spring morning was like.

Therefore, as we read this poem, it feels like we can hear the singing of the birds, feel the fresh air in the morning, smell the sweet fragrance of the flowers and naturally imagine the activities of the poet.

Inspiration

Catching the sounds of spring (the twitter of the birds, the sounds of the breeze and the rain) to express what the poet felt is the main characteristic of this poem. With this thought, I created a piece of music to go with this short poem in 2005.

But, when I wanted to paint a picture to match the artistic conception of this poem in 2011, I had a new idea. I thought that the last two lines (夜来风雨声，花落知多少。) yè lái fēng yǔ shēng, huā luò zhī duō shǎo—In the night's wind and rain, how many flowers have fallen—could not only have been the thought of the poet but also have been what the birds were singing.

Therefore, I painted two paintings to match this idea as my assignments at China Central Academy of Fine Arts and at Chinese National Academy of Arts in 2011 and 2012. Let the birds open their mouths to sing and ask how many flowers have fallen in the wind and rain last night.

What do you think of my imagination? Do you agree with me?

Vocabulary

春晓　　chūn xiǎo　　the title of the poem, which means a spring morning

春　　chūn　　*n.*　　spring

晓　　xiǎo　　*n./v.*　　dawn, daybreak

孟浩然　　mèng hào rán　　a famous poet in the Tang Dynasty

唐　　táng　　*n.*　　the Tang Dynasty（618 – 907）

春眠不觉晓　　chūn mián bù jué xiǎo　　Sleeping on a spring night, I've missed the dawn.

眠　　mián　　*v.*　　sleep

不觉　　bù jué　　*v.*　　do not know, do not realize

不　　bù　　*adv.*　　no, not

觉　　jué　　*v.*　　feel, realize

处处闻啼鸟　　chù chù wén tí niǎo　　Everywhere I hear the songs of birds.

处处　　chù chù　　*adv.*　　everywhere

闻　　wén　　*v.*　　hear, listen to

啼　　tí　　*v.*　　chirp, twitter, crow

鸟　　niǎo　　*n.*　　bird

夜来风雨声　　yè lái fēng yǔ shēng　　In the night's wind and rain.

夜来　　yè lái　　*n.*　　night, here means last night

风　　fēng　　*n.*　　wind, breeze

雨　　yǔ　　*v./n.*　　rain

声　　shēng　　*n.*　　sound

花落知多少　　huā luò zhī duō shǎo　　How many flowers have fallen?

花　　huā　　*n.*　　flower, blossom

落　　luò　　*v.*　　drop, fall

知　　zhī　　*v.*　　know, realize

多少　　duō shǎo　　*adv.*　　number,　　how many

春眠不觉晓，处处闻啼鸟。夜来风雨声，花落知多少。

chūn mián bù jué xiǎo, chù chù wén tí niǎo。 yè lái fēng yǔ shēng,
huā luò zhī duō shǎo。

Sleeping on a spring night, I've missed the dawn.

Everywhere I hear the songs of birds.

In the night's wind and rain,

How many flowers have fallen?

02. 惠崇春江晚景—Inscription on Hui Chong's Painting "An Evening Scene on a Spring River"

惠崇春江晚景—huì chóng chūn jiāng wǎn jǐng

宋—sòng　苏轼—sū shì

竹外桃花三两枝—zhú wài táo huā sān liǎng zhī,

春江水暖鸭先知—chūn jiāng shuǐ nuǎn yā xiān zhī。

蒌蒿满地芦芽短—lóu hāo mǎn dì lú yá duǎn,

正是河豚欲上时—zhèng shì hé tún yù shàng shí。

"An Evening Scene on a Spring River"

By Su Shi　Song Dynasty

Beyond the bamboo grove, there're a few twigs of peach blossoms.

The spring river water gets warm, ducks know it first.

Wormwood herb is everywhere, and reeds' buds just grow.

It is the time when globefish will swim upstream.

6

About the Poet

Su Shi 苏轼 sū shì (1037 – 1101) is recognized as having attained the highest level of achievement in literature in Song Dynasty (960 – 1279) for his outstanding contribution to poetry, lyrics and essays. He was also a great calligraphist and a famous artist.

Su Shi was from Mei Shan, Sichuan Province. He had a very good educational background and he got a name with his father and his younger brother as the San (three) Su.

He was a successful candidate in the highest imperial examination and achieved much in his official positions.

As a poet, his fame and reputation were similar to that of Huang Tingjian and together they were known as "Su and Huang".

As a lyricist, Su Shi attained the highest level of achievement in the Northern Song (960 – 1127) with regard to both content and form. He was the originator of the genre of poetry known as "Bold and Unconstrained" (豪放派). He and Xin Qiji, the other great poet in the Southern Song (1127 – 1279), were known as "Su and Xin".

As an essayist, Su Shi was very good at writing essays. He was one of the eight greatest masters in Tang and Song. He had the same reputation as Ou Yangxiu and together they were known as "Ou and Su".

As a calligraphist, he was famous for his running hand and regular script. As an artist, his favorite subject was bamboo.

Su Shi was not only famous for writing, painting and handwriting, he also had his own theories about literature and art. He emphasized that literature should be a unique, expressive force and have artistic value.

He has left more than 4,000 poems, about 340 lyrics and many essays to the world.

This poem was inscribed on a painting by a monk and artist named Hui Chong. In a few lines, it paints a beautiful picture of the early spring scenery south of the Yangtze River.

The practice of inscribing poems on paintings started in the Song Dynasty, and these inscribed poems are known as Ti Hua Shi（题画诗）—poems on paintings.

I am sure that in China, instead of remembering the title, most people just remember the most famous line of the poem: "chūn jiāng shuǐ nuǎn yā xiān zhī—ducks would be the first to know when the spring river water gets warm".

Enjoy the Poem

The first line: 竹外桃花三两枝 zhú wài táo huā sān liǎng zhī—Beyond the bamboo grove, there're a few twigs of peach blossoms.

While, on the surface, this line describes a scenery and does not mention the word "spring", it does, in fact, keep close to the subject of "spring", particularly "early spring". We know this from the simple words in the line:

—The bamboo grove is sparse, we can see the peach blossoms behind it.

—There are just a few branches of peach blossoms beyond the bamboo, because it is not the season that peach blossoms are in full bloom.

—The green or yellow bamboo and the pink peach blossoms show us that spring is on its way.

The second line: 春江水暖鸭先知 chūn jiāng shuǐ nuǎn yā xiān zhī—The spring river water gets warm, ducks know it first.

Spring has come quietly; it is getting warm, but not everyone can feel it yet. With a wonderful imagination, this line tells us that the ducks in the water feel the warmth before human beings in the early spring. The meaning, which is difficult to express, has been shown to us vividly at once.

Therefore, this line has been a well-known line in the history of

Chinese poetry since it was written.

The third line: 蒌蒿满地芦芽短 lóu hāo mǎn dì lú yá duǎn—Wormwood herb is everywhere, and reeds' buds just grow.

Because it is the early spring, the wormwood herb is growing everywhere, but the reeds are still short. Both of these plants—wormwood herb and reeds' buds—capture the imagination of the poet, and so we have the last line:

The fourth line: 正是河豚欲上时 zhèng shì hé tún yù shàng shí—It is the time when globefish will swim upstream (another version: It is the time when the globefish will be ready for the market).

Since people who live along the Yangtze River usually cook globefish with wormwood, reeds' buds and Chinese cabbage, the previous line naturally made the poet think of the globefish.

Apart from its famous line "春江水暖鸭先知 chūn jiāng shuǐ nuǎn yā xiān zhī—The spring river water gets warm, ducks know it first", the combination of the actual scenery and the imagination to describe the early spring, is the main character of this poem.

For example:

The first line describes the actual scenery, the second line is a combination of scenery and imagination, the third line is again a description of scenery and the fourth line is pure imagination, and so all these elements are combined together and the whole poem is full of the beautiful breath of life.

Inspiration

After reading this poem, a strong feeling I got is that a good art work can not be seperated from real life. Life is always the source of the creation of art. If Su Shi did not understand the nature, the social customs and the way of life in the regions of south of the Yangtze River, he would not have been able to write the wonderful line "the spring river water gets warm, ducks know it first", and he would not have been able to write the lines like "it is the time when globefish will swim upstream or it is the time when the globefish will be ready for the market".

If we want to be good artists, apart from studying in schools and learning from teachers and books, we also have to go into the nature and the society, to learn and to absorb something wonderful from the myriads of things. Do you agree?

I learned the line "春江水暖鸭先知 chūn jiāng shuǐ nuǎn yā xiān zhī—The spring river water gets warm, ducks know it first" in my childhood, studied the whole of the poem in my college days and it wasn't until 2003 that I painted a picture to express the meaning of this line, but at that time I had no idea how to match a painting with a poem.

It wasn't until 2005 that I first composed a piece of music to go with the poem, and then in 2007 I created a painting to go with the music and the poem. Then in 2011 and 2012, at Chinese National Academy of Arts, as one of my assignments, I painted and then re-painted a picture for this poem consciously.

Vocabulary

惠崇春江晚景　　huì chóng chūn jiāng wǎn jǐng　the title of the poem

Hui Chong is the name of a friend of Su Shi. He is a famous artist and a monk. He is good at poetry and drawing. Chun Jiang Wan Jing means "An Evening Scene on a Spring River", it is a famous work of Hui Chong.

Su Shi wrote this poem on the painting in accordance with the meaning of the picture.

惠崇　huì chóng　*n.*　name of a friend of Su Shi

春　chūn　*n.*　spring

江　jiāng　*n.*　river, here it means the Yangtze River—in ancient

Chinese language, "river" usually refers to the Yangtze River

晚　wǎn　*adj.*　evening, night, late

景　jǐng　*n.*　scene, scenery, landscape, view

苏轼　sū shì　name of one of the most famous literary figures in Song Dynasty (960 – 1279)

竹外桃花三两枝　zhú wài táo huā sān liǎng zhī　Beyond the bamboo grove, there are a few twigs of peach blossoms.

竹　zhú　*n.*　bamboo

外　wài　*adv.*　outside, beyond

桃花　táo huā　*n.*　peach blossom

三　sān　*numeral*　three

两　liǎng　*numeral*　two

枝　zhī　*n.*　branch, twig

春江水暖鸭先知　chūn jiāng shuǐ nuǎn yā xiān zhī　The spring river water gets warm, ducks know it first.

水　shuǐ　*n.*　water, river, sea, stream

暖　nuǎn　*adj./v.*　warm , here means "get warm"

鸭　yā　*n.*　duck

先　xiān　*adv.*　first, earlier, here means the earliest

知　zhī　*v.*　know, realize, perceive

蒌蒿满地芦芽短　lóu hāo mǎn dì lú yá duǎn　Wormwood herb is everywhere, and reeds' buds just grow.

蒌蒿　lóu hāo　*n.*　Indian wormwood herb

满地　mǎn dì　*adv.*　all over, everywhere

芦芽　lú yá　*n.*　bud of reed

短　duǎn　*adj.*　short, here it means that the buds of the reeds just emerge

正是河豚欲上时　zhèng shì hé tún yù shàng shí　It is the time when globefish will swim upstream.

正　zhèng　*adv.*　just

是　　shì　*v.*　be, is, are

河豚　　hé tún　*n.*　globefish, a kind of fish　The taste of its meat is good, but its liver and ovaries are poisonous. Every spring they swim upstream and spawn in the fresh water.

欲　　yù　*v.*　want, wish, will

上　　shàng　*adv.*　go up, here it means upstream—the globefish will swim upstream to spawn

时　　shí　*adv.*　when, time

竹外桃花三两枝，春江水暖鸭先知；蒌蒿满地芦芽短，正是河豚欲上时。zhú wài táo huā sān liǎng zhī, chūn jiāng shuǐ nuǎn yā xiān zhī。lóu hāo mǎn dì lú yá duǎn, zhèng shì hé tún yù shàng shí。

Beyond the bamboo grove, there're a few twigs of peach blossoms.

The spring river water gets warm, ducks know it first.

Wormwood herb is everywhere, and reeds' buds just grow.

It is the time when globefish will swim upstream.

03. 咏鹅—Singing About Geese

咏鹅—yǒng é

唐—táng　　骆宾王—luò bīn wáng

鹅，鹅，鹅—é，é，é，

曲项向天歌—qǔ（qū）xiàng xiàng tiān gē。

白毛浮绿水—bái máo fú lù shuǐ，

红掌拨清波—hóng zhǎng bō qīng bō。

Singing About Geese

By Luo Binwang　　Tang Dynasty

Geese, geese, geese,

Bend their necks to sing to the sky.

White feathers are floating on the green water,

Red feet are paddling the clear waves.

About the Poet

Luo Binwang 骆宾王 luò bīn wáng（619 – 687）was born in Yiwu in today's Zhejiang Province. He was from a poor family, but he could write poems when he was just 7 years old, and so he was called a "Wonder Child".

Luo Binwang was a famous poet in the early Tang Dynasty, and he was one of the Chu Tang Si Jie（初唐四杰）—four greatest poets（the other three were Wang Bo, Yang Jiong and Lu Zhaolin）of the early Tang Dynasty. In 684, when Xu Jingye started a war against Empress Wu Zetian, he wrote a famous call to arms *Wei Xu Jingye Tao Wu Zhao Xi* （《为徐敬业讨武曌檄》）—a declaration of war against Wu Zhao on behalf of Xu Jingye, in which he put the Empress Wu Zetian in the dock and read out her crimes. This became one of the best calls to arms in Chinese history such that even Empress Wu Zetian herself said it was the fault of her prime minister that a person with such talent had got unnoticed and had come down in the world with no opportunity to develop himself. After Xu Jingye failed, Luo Binwang's whereabouts was unknown and there were two accounts of what might have happened to him. One version said that he was killed, the other version said that he became a monk.

Stories About Geese

In ancient China, some princes and nobles raised geese as guard birds. They used watchdogs in a similar way.

It is said, in Jin Dynasty（265 – 420）, the Sage of Calligraphy— Mr. Wang Xizhi（303 – 361）quite loved geese. No matter where there were good geese, he was eager to see them, or buy and raise them.

Mr. Wang Xizhi enjoyed the qualities of geese—they do not hurry when they walk. They are leisurely and carefree when they swim. He thought that to raise geese would not only edify peoples' good sentiment, but through learning about the posture and the attitude of the geese, it also could help people to learn that something natural is just the most beautiful and to understand the secret of calligraphy's writing movements.

He thought, when we hold a Chinese brush, the forefinger should be like the head of a goose, lifted and a little bent; when we ran the brush, we should work like a goose's webbed feet paddling the water, then we could focus on the artistic conception of what was being written.

Here are two stories about how he loved geese:

One morning, Mr. Wang Xizhi and his son (a calligrapher) Wang Xianzhi visited Shaoxi. As their boat went by Xiang Village, he was so attracted by the lovely style of a family of white geese which were waddling and dillydallying along the river bank that he wanted to buy them.

Then Mr. Wang Xizhi asked the Taoist monk nearby if he would sell them to him. The Taoist monk responded, "if you want them, please write a *Huang Ting Jing* (a Taoist scripture) for us. " Since Mr. Wang Xizhi really loved the geese, he happily agreed.

Another story:

Mr. Wang Xizhi lived in Lan Ting in today's Zhejiang Province. He built a pool specially for raising geese and named it "鹅池 é chí" — Goose Pool. By his Goose Pool he built a stele and a pavilion.

It is said that, one day, Mr. Wang Xizhi was writing the characters "鹅池 é chí" —Goose Pool. When he had just completed the first character, "鹅 é" —Goose, a minister came to Wang's home with a decree from the emperor, Wang had to put down his brush and went out to accept the decree of the emperor. His son, Mr. Wang Xianzhi who was also a great calligrapher found that his father had just written one character, "鹅 é", so he took up the brush and wrote the other word, "池 chí".

Both the characters are very similar and harmonious. Since then, the story of the two characters on the same stele written by the father and the son has become an anecdote and passed down through the ages, and the Goose Pool has been a scenic spot for tourists for about 1,500 years.

Enjoy the Poem

This poem was written when Luo Binwang was 7 years old, about 100 years after Wang Xizhi passed away.

From the angle of a child, seeing how the geese swim and play in the water, it is very lively and vivid.

The first two lines：鹅，鹅，鹅，曲项向天歌 é, é, é, qǔ xiàng xiàng tiān gē—Geese, geese, geese, bend their necks to sing to the sky.

These lines describe the sounds of the geese, their features and how they sing. They sing by bending their necks, instead of extending their necks, which is quite an exact expression.

The last two lines：白毛浮绿水，红掌拨清波 bái máo fú lǜ shuǐ, hóng zhǎng bō qīng bō —White feathers are floating on the green water, red (webbed) feet are paddling the clear waves.

These two lines catch the activities and the colors of the geese, to write about the scene and how the geese swim in the water.

With the verbs "浮 fú" —float and "拨 bō" —paddle, to describe the activities of the geese, how they swim or play in the water, with the phrases "white feathers", "red feet", "green water" and "clear waves", to write about what the geese look like and where they are playing, these lines create a beautiful picture with bright colors and light-footed activities. The three words "鹅，鹅，鹅 é, é, é" —geese, geese, geese " in the first line add sounds to the picture, so we can not only see the geese on the water, but also, we can hear the little poet's sounds, or the sounds of the geese. I mean that we can imagine the three words "鹅，鹅，鹅 é, é, é " are the sounds uttered by the little poet, and we can also imagine they are sounds of the geese themselves, which are their cries.

The whole of the little poem is joyous, natural and lifelike. It sees and sings about geese from a child's viewpoint, very simple and full of childlike fun, so it is very popular in China. Since it was created, it has been enjoyed by Chinese children and adults. Many people are able to recite it before they enter elementary school.

Inspiration

When I read this poem once more today, I can not help thinking how such a young child could absorb things in such details and create such a wonderful poem that has been handed down through generations for about 1,400 years. Apart from his talent, maybe it was because he had childlike innocence?

With this idea, I am thinking, if an artist wants to create something natural, fresh and beautiful, besides having some artistic skills, maybe he should also have a childlike innocence inside. If we put aside utilitarianism and observe the world with a pure heart and impersonal attitude, can we then really pick up something true and objective and so create something transcendent, elegant and miraculous?

With an appreciative heart for the poet, I translated this poem in April, 2005 and created a piece of music for it in October, 2006. As my assignments at Chinese National Academy of Arts, I painted three paintings to match the music and the poem in 2011 and 2012.

Vocabulary

咏鹅　yǒng é　the title of the poem by Luo Binwang, meaning singing about geese

咏　yǒng　*v.* chant; intone

鹅　é　*n.* goose

骆宾王　luò bīn wáng　a poet in the Tang Dynasty

鹅，鹅，鹅　é, é, é　Goose, goose, goose. / Geese, geese, geese.

曲项向天歌　qǔ xiàng xiàng tiān gē　Bend their necks to sing to the sky.

曲　qǔ　*v.*　bend

项　xiàng　*n.*　neck

向　xiàng　*prep.*　to, towards

天　tiān　*n.*　sky, heaven

歌　gē　*v. /n.*　　*v.*　sing , *n.*　song

白毛浮绿水　bái máo fú lǜ shuǐ　White feathers are floating on the green water.

白　bái　*adj.*　white

毛　máo　*n.*　feather, hair

浮　fú　*v.*　float

绿　lǜ　*adj.*　green

水　shuǐ　*n.*　water, river, sea, stream

红掌拨清波　hóng zhǎng bō qīng bō　Red（webbed）feet are paddling the clear waves.

红　hóng　*adj.*　red

掌　zhǎng　*n.*　webbed foot, sole

拨　bō　*v.*　paddle, row

清　qīng　*adj.*　clear

波　bō　*n.*　wave

鹅，鹅，鹅，曲项向天歌。白毛浮绿水，红掌拨清波。

é，é，é，qǔ xiàng xiàng tiān gē。bái máo fú lǜ shuǐ，hóng zhǎng bō qīng bō。

Geese, geese, geese,

Bend their necks to sing to the sky.

White feathers are floating on the green water,

Red feet are paddling the clear waves.

04. 小池—A Little Pool

小池—xiǎo chí

宋—sòng　杨万里—yáng wàn lǐ

泉眼无声惜细流—quán yǎn wú shēng xī xì liú,

树阴照水爱晴柔—shù yīn zhào shuǐ ài qíng róu。

小荷才露尖尖角—xiǎo hé cái lù jiān jiān jiǎo,

早有蜻蜓立上头—zǎo yǒu qīng tíng lì shàng tóu。

A Little Pool

By Yang Wanli　Song Dynasty

The silent mouth of a spring cherishes the thin streamlet,

The shadow of the trees is reflected in the water, it loves the scene in the sunshine.

A little lotus leaf just appears with a sharp tip,

Quickly a dragonfly lands on it.

About the Poet

Yang Wanli 杨万里 yáng wàn lǐ (1127 – 1206) was from Jizhou in today's Jiangxi Province. He was a successful candidate in the highest imperial examinations in 1154 and was a good official.

Yang Wanli was a patriot. Politically, he insisted on fighting against the aggression of the Jin (1115 – 1234), a northern nation. But his political views were not accepted by the Court and after trying many times, he became disheartened and withdrew from society and lived in solitude for 15 years until he died with a sorrowful heart.

Yang Wanli was a famous poet in the Southern Song Dynasty (1127 – 1279) —There were two phases of Song Dynasty (960 – 1279), the Northern Song (960 – 1127) and the Southern Song (1127 – 1279). He was one of four greatest masters of the Southern Song and has a same reputation as You Mao, Fan Chengda and Lu You in the history of Chinese literature.

Yang Wanli wrote over 20,000 poems of which more than 4,200 still exist.

Enjoy the Poem

Xiao Chi — A Little Pool is a poem about a small but interesting scene on a beautiful summer's day. Through depicting the mouth of a spring, a little streamlet, the shadow of a tree, several lotus leaves and a lovely dragonfly, it forms a lively picture of a little pool, showing the harmonious relationship among things in nature.

The first two lines: 泉眼无声惜细流，树阴照水爱晴柔 quán yǎn wú shēng xī xì liú, shù yīn zhào shuǐ ài qíng róu— The silent mouth of a spring "cherishes" the thin streamlet, the shadow of a tree is reflected in the water, it "loves" the soft view on the sunny day.

With wonderful imagination and personifying words, the poet endowed natural things with the life and the attributes of human beings: The mouth of the spring *cherishes* the streamlet, so that it *lets* the water flow silently and thinly; the shadow of the tree *loves* the soft and fine view in the water, so that *it* is reflected in the water too. These two lines create a little, exquisite and delightful scene.

The last two lines: 小荷才露尖尖角，早有蜻蜓立上头 xiǎo hé cái lù jiān jiān jiǎo, zǎo yǒu qīng tíng lì shàng tóu—The pointed tip of a slim lotus leaf just appears before opening her body, and quickly a dragonfly lands on it.

Just like a good photographer who is able to snap some interesting picture, the two lines capture the moment when the pointed tip of a lotus leaf appears, a dragonfly immediately lands on it, and write about how both of the lotus leaf and the dragonfly "enjoy and rely on" each other.

Yang Wanli was quite interested in the natural landscape, and very often he used a clear and lively tone, an easy and popular language, to describe everyday and common views; he was especially good at capturing the character of the views and their transient moments, his poems paint some interesting pictures and they are full of strong breath of life.

With this writing style, no matter how small the things were that he wrote about, whether a little flower, a little worm or a little bird, they all have the same feelings and thoughts as people, with a vivacious, lovely, witty and humorous style.

Mr. Wang Guowei (1877 – 1927), a versatile scholar who made important contributions to the studies of ancient history, epigraphy, philology, vernacular literature and literary theory said:

"The subject of a poem can be big or small; we should not judge whether a poem is excellent or otherwise from the largeness or smallness of its subject. "

Relating to the title " A Little Pool", every thing in the poem is small, but full of the feelings of humans: The mouth of the spring is small, its stream is thin, so it seems that the spring does not want it to flow out of the spring mouth; the shadow of a tree is reflected into the water, because it loves the soft sunny sky that is also reflected in the water, and wants to be with the blue sky; the lotus leaf is small, it has not opened its body, and just appears a little sharp tip; the dragonfly is small but clever, as soon as it finds the little tip of the lotus leaf, it lands on it at once... No matter whether a mouth of a spring, the shade of a tree or a dragonfly, all the things in the poem are alive and have feelings just like human beings; each line is just like a picture. Many pictures together create a beautiful artistic conception.

China is a poetic country. In our daily life, we often use some lines to make our language more implicative and easier to understand. Nowadays when we want to say that only a small part of something is visible or just appears while most of it is still hidden or has not yet showed, we often say "小荷才露尖尖角 xiǎo hé cái lù jiān jiān jiǎo—The pointed tip of a slim lotus leaf just appears before opening her body ". The little lotus leaf is often used to describe someone who is just beginning to show his ability and talent; the dragonfly is just like someone who admires such a person.

Inspiration

To catch those small but interesting split second in nature and to create a wonderful artistic conception with some personifying but exact words is the main character of this poem. It is also the general requirement of an artist. If we would like to be good artists, we must have a good pair of eyes that are able to find something special and beautiful among what are simple things in most people's eyes, and to note them down in some artistic styles.

In contemporary society, many people are very busy and they rush around having no time to pay attention to the beauty that surrounds them, and they sometimes complain that there is no, or a lack of beauty in their lives.

In fact, there are beautiful things everywhere, every tree by the roadside, every blade of grass in the corner, every flower by our foot, or every cloud over our heads is beautiful if we observe it carefully. Everything has life and even some feelings if you care for it and feel or think from its point of view. "There is not a lack of beauty in the world, but a lack of eyes being able to find beauty in daily life. "

Anyway, an artist, maybe not only needs a pair of eyes that can find beauty, but also should be able to express the beauty by the most suitable artistic method, to capture the transient beauty, and express it quickly. Therefore, we have to improve ourselves on both insight and skills every day. Do you agree?

With much enjoyment of the poem, I translated it and composed a piece of music for it seperately in 2006. Then I learned to paint two pictures for it in 2010 and 2012 at China Central Academy of Fine Arts and Chinese National Academy of Arts.

Vocabulary

小池　xiǎo chí　*n.*　the title of the poem, which means a little lotus pool

小　xiǎo　*adj.*　small, little, young

池　chí　*n.*　pond, pool

杨万里　yáng wàn lǐ　a poet's name in the Song Dynasty

宋　sòng　*n.*　the Song Dynasty (960 – 1279)

泉眼无声惜细流　quán yǎn wú shēng xī xì liú　The silent mouth of a spring cherishes the thin streamlet (and lets it flow into the pond quietly and gently) .

泉眼　quán yǎn　*n.*　the mouth of a spring

泉　quán　*n.*　spring, underground water

眼　yǎn　*n.*　eye, small hole, here it means the mouth of a spring

无声　wú shēng　*n. /adj.*　no sound, silent

无　wú　*v.*　there is no, not have

声　shēng　*n.*　sound, voice

惜　xī　*v.*　cherish

细流　xì liú　*n.*　streamlet

细　xì　*adv.*　thin

流　liú　*n.* / *v.*　*n.* stream, *v.* flow

树阴照水爱晴柔　shù yīn zhào shuǐ ài qíng róu　The shadow of the trees is reflected in the water, for it loves the soft scene in the sunshine in the water.

树阴　shù yīn　*n.*　the shadow of trees

树　shù　*n.*　tree

阴　yīn　*n.*　shade, shadow

照　zhào　*v.*　reflect, mirror

水　shuǐ　*n.*　water, river, sea, stream

爱　ài　*v.*　love, like

晴　qíng　*adj.*　fine, sunshine

柔　róu　*adj.*　soft, gentle

小荷才露尖尖角　xiǎo hé cái lù jiān jiān jiǎo　A little lotus leaf just appears with her pointed/sharp tip.

荷　hé　*n.*　lotus, water lily, here it means lotus leaf

才　cái　*adv.*　just

露　lù　*v.*　reveal, appear

尖尖　jiān jiān　*adj.*　pointed, sharp

角　jiǎo　*n.*　horn, here it means the pointed / sharp tip of the leaf of lotus

早有蜻蜓立上头　zǎo yǒu qīng tíng lì shàng tóu　Quickly a dragonfly lands on it.

早　zǎo　*adv.* / *n.*　early

有　yǒu　*v.*　there is / are, have

蜻蜓　qīng tíng　*n.*　dragonfly

立　　lì　*v.*　stand up

上头　　shàng tou　*n.*　over, above

泉眼无声惜细流，树阴照水爱晴柔。小荷才露尖尖角，早有蜻蜓立上头。quán yǎn wú shēng xī xì liú, shù yīn zhào shuǐ ài qíng róu。xiǎo hé cái lù jiān jiān jiǎo, zǎo yǒu qīng tíng lì shàng tóu。

The silent mouth of a spring cherishes the thin streamlet,

The shadow of the trees is reflected in the water, it loves the scene in the sunshine.

A little lotus leaf just appears with a sharp tip,

Quickly a dragonfly lands on it.

05. 江畔独步寻花—Finding Flowers Alone by the River

江畔独步寻花—jiāng pàn dú bù xún huā

唐—táng　杜甫—dù fǔ

黄四娘家花满蹊—huáng sì niáng jiā huā mǎn xī,

千朵万朵压枝低—qiān duǒ wàn duǒ yā zhī dī。

留连戏蝶时时舞—liú lián xì dié shí shí wǔ,

自在娇莺恰恰啼—zì zài jiāo yīng qià qià tí。

Finding Flowers Alone by the River

By Du Fu　Tang Dynasty

Ms. Huang Si's path is covered with blossoms,

Numerous flowers are bending the branches low.

Playful butterflies are dancing, unwilling to leave,

Carefree cute birds are singing "qia qia".

About the Poet

Du Fu 杜甫 dù fǔ(712 – 770) was born in today's Henan Province during Tang Dynasty (618 – 907). He is one of the greatest poets in the history of Chinese poetry.

Du Fu had a very good home education; he had been writing poetry since he was 5 and started to learn Chinese calligraphy when he was 9. He communicated with adults through poetry from the age of 15 or 16.

His first travels were in Wu and Yue—today's Zhejiang and Jiangsu provinces and he knew another equally great poet of Tang Dynasty—Li Bai at the age of about 20. At that time, his poems were very positive and full of dreams.

When he was 22 years old, he failed in the imperial examinations but he stayed in the capital Chang'an City—Today's Xi'an for about 10 years, living a very poor life, and he got to know much about the lives of common people. His poetry entered into a new phase, that was Realism.

As a follower of Confucian philosophy, Du Fu cared for the future and fate of the country and he wished to have an opportunity to work for the country; however, it wasn't until he was 44 years old did he have the opportunity to become an officer.

In 755, the Rebellion of An and Shi (755 – 763) led the country into a civil war lasting for about 8 years. During that time, Du Fu became a fugitive, experienced a harder and poorer life and his poetry reached its highest peak. In 770, when he was 58 years old and on his way back to his hometown, Du Fu died on a boat.

Du Fu experienced the decline of the Tang Dynasty from its most prosperous times and his poetry reflected the whole of this process, so people said his poetry was "Poetry of Historic Significance". Meanwhile, he developed the traditional Chinese poetry forms. Either long or short poems, he could write them excellently.

Du Fu's poetry has been influential among poets for about 1, 200 years. There are about 1, 400 of his poems still in existence.

Enjoy the Poem

This poem was written in 761. After experiencing the hardship in the Rebellion of An and Shi which started in Central China, Du Fu went to Chengdu, Sichuan, where he built a thatched cottage by a stream in the Western Suburbs of Chengdu so that he had a resting place temporarily. With an easy heart, he walked by the river, enjoying the beauty of flowers in the warm spring, and then he wrote seven poems of Qi Jue（七绝）（a four-line poem with seven characters each line and a strict tonal pattern and rhyming scheme）.

Jiang Pan Du Bu Xun Hua is the 6th poem of the group of Qi Jue.

The first two lines：黄四娘家花满蹊，千朵万朵压枝低 huáng sì niáng jiā huā mǎn xī, qiān duǒ wàn duǒ yā zhī dī—Ms. Huang Si's path is covered with blossoms, numerous flowers are bending the branches low.

The first line writes about the place where the poet found the flowers. They are just on the road by Ms. Huang Si's house and have covered the road already. The second line describes how big and many the flowers are. They are tier upon tier, so that they have bent the branches low. Both of the two lines emphasize the flowers' quantity and size, and they have covered the road and bent the branches.

The last two lines：留连戏蝶时时舞，自在娇莺恰恰啼 liú lián xì dié shí shí wǔ, zì zài jiāo yīng qià qià tí—Playful butterflies are dancing, unwilling to leave, carefree cute birds are singing "qia qia".

They have attracted the butterflies " 留连 liú lián" —lingering and dancing over them, not wanting to leave; they fascinated the yellow birds singing among or over them.

By writing about the actions of the butterflies and the sounds of the birds, the poet hints to us how beautiful the flowers are.

The phrase "时时舞 shí shí wǔ" —often dance writes about how the butterflies dance; and " '恰恰' 啼 qià qià tí" —sing "qia qia" writes what the birds sing, with the visual language, and helps us "see" a beautiful view, "smell" the fragrance of the flowers, "listen to" the wonderful sounds and "feel" the emotion of happiness. These not only endue the little poem with a dynamic feeling, but also give the poem a very bright and fluent rhythm.

Because the poet himself was happy at the time to find the flowers, he felt everything in the happiness, the lovely butterflies dancing for him and carefree cute yellow birds singing for him.

Through empathizing the poet's feeling towards the butterflies and birds, endowing them with human feelings, this poem blends the object and subject, natural scenery and human feeling together, and creates its own artistic result, brings us to the little path of 1, 252 years ago, helps us to enjoy the beautiful natural scenery as well as shares the poet's feeling of delight.

Inspiration

Projecting the poet's happy feelings onto the natural things that he was writing about is the main characteristic of this poem.

The transfer of the human feeling to some object, can help us create some wonderful art work, such as this poem. However, in the real world, we should never bring any personal feeling into work. Especially, we should not transfer any bad emotion into management art.

Years ago, a friend gave up her opportunity to study abroad, because she wanted to do her best for the company that she had given her best time to. Instead of going to the consulate to get her visa at the appointed time, she wrote a work report over several weekends and many nights. With an excited heart, she gave her report to her boss on the Monday morning. Instead of getting any appreciation, her boss frowned. With so much surprise, disappointment and frustration, she re-made the appointment at the consulate, got her visa and left for the other side of the ocean.

Later, her boss apologized to her and explained that he had been in big trouble that day, so that he could not help losing his temper with the one who entered his office first. However, things could not be retrieved.

Transfering feeling is a good method in art creation; but it is not a good thing to take personal feeling to work. Do you agree?

Untill now, I still remember how I recited this poem with an enjoyable heart on a little path in the campus of my first university on a sunny morning. Then I translated this poem into English and created a piece of music for it in 2006. Since then, I have created more than 10 paintings for it. But now, I would like to show you the last one that is my assignment at Chinese National Academy of Arts in 2012.

Vocabulary

江畔独步寻花　　jiāng pàn dú bù xún huā　　the title of the poem which means looking for flowers while going for a walk by the river alone

江畔　jiāng pàn　*phrase*　by the river

江　jiāng　*n.*　river, here it means the Yangtse River —in ancient Chinese language, "River" means the Yangtse River

畔　pàn　*n.*　bank, side

独　dú　*adv.*　lonely, alone, solely

步　bù　*v.*　go on foot; walk

寻　xún　*v.*　look for, seek

花　huā　*n.*　flower, blossom

唐　táng　*n.*　the Tang Dynasty（618 – 907）

杜甫 dù fǔ（712 – 770）a poet's name in the Tang Dynasty

黄四娘家花满蹊　　huáng sì niáng jiā huā mǎn xī　　Ms. Huang Si's path is covered with blossoms.

黄四娘　huáng sì niáng　name of person

黄　huáng　*adj. /n.*　*adj.*　yellow　*n.*　a Chinese family name

四娘　sì niáng　*n.*　the first name of the lady in the poem, which means the lady who is listed as 4th in the family

四　sì *numeral*　four

娘　niáng　*n.*　mother, mum; a form of address for an elderly married woman; a young woman; young lady

家　jiā　*n.*　home, family

满　mǎn　*v.*　all over, full

蹊　xī　*n.*　footpath, path

千朵万朵压枝低　qiān duǒ wàn duǒ yā zhī dī　Numerous flowers are bending the branches low.

千朵万朵　qiān duǒ wàn duǒ　*phrase*　thousands and ten thousands of flowers, to express the meaning of "many", "numerous"

千　qiān　*quantifier*　thousand

朵　duǒ　*measure word*　It has no meaning, but helps to express how many flowers, clouds, or things like flowers and clouds, such as a flower, a cloud.

万　wàn　*quantifier*　ten thousand

压　yā　*v.*　weigh down, press, push down

枝　zhī　*n.*　branch, twig

低　dī　*adj.*　low

留连戏蝶时时舞　liú lián xì dié shí shí wǔ　Playful butterflies are dancing, unwilling to leave.

留连　liú lián　*adv/adj.*　linger, lingering, unwilling to leave

戏　xì　*adj.*　playful

蝶　dié　*n.*　butterfly

时时　shí shí　*adv.*　often; from time to time

舞　wǔ　*v.*　dance

自在娇莺恰恰啼　zì zài jiāo yīng qià qià tí　Carefree cute birds (warbler; oriole) are singing "qia qia".

自在　zì zài　*adv.*　free, comfortable

娇　jiāo　*adj.*　tender, lovely, cute

莺　yīng　*n.*　warbler; oriole

恰恰　qià qià　*n.*　the sound of the birds

啼　tí　*v.*　twitter, crow, chirp

黄四娘家花满蹊，千朵万朵压枝低。留连戏蝶时时舞，自在娇莺恰恰啼。huáng sì niáng jiā huā mǎn xī, qiān duǒ wàn duǒ yā zhī dī。liú lián xì dié shí shí wǔ, zì zài jiāo yīng qià qià tí。

Ms. Huang Si's path is covered with blossoms,

Numerous flowers are bending the branches low.

Playful butterflies are dancing, unwilling to leave,

Carefree cute birds are singing "qia qia".

06. 望月怀远—Looking at the Moon & Missing Someone Far Away

望月怀远—wàng yuè huái yuǎn

唐— táng   张九龄—zhāng jiǔ líng

海上生明月—hǎi shàng shēng míng yuè,

天涯共此时—tiān yá gòng cǐ shí。

情人怨遥夜—qíng rén yuàn yáo yè,

竟夕起相思—jìng xī qǐ xiāng sī。

灭烛怜光满—miè zhú lián guāng mǎn,

披衣觉露滋—pī yī jué lù zī。

不堪盈手赠—bù kān yíng shǒu zèng,

还寝梦佳期—huán qǐn mèng jiā qī。

Looking at the Moon & Missing Someone Far Away

By Zhang Jiuling   Tang Dynasty

A bright moon is rising over the sea,

We see her from afar at the same time.

Sweethearts complain the night is too long,

Lovesick, we stay up all night.

You put out the candle, go out to see the moon.

You cover with clothes but you still feel the wet of dew.

Since you can not hold some moonlight to me,

You decide to go back to sleep and wish to meet me in your dream.

About the Poet

Zhang Jiuling 张九龄 zhāng jiǔ líng（678 – 740）, was born in Qujiang（in modern Shaoguan, Guangdong）. He was a prominent prime minister, and served as chancellor during the reign of Emperor Xuanzong. He became known for his ability to understand people's talents and he insisted on using talented people as officials, so he had a good reputation as a "Virtuous Prime Minister".

Zhang Jiuling was also one of the noted and transitional poets between Prosperous and Flourishing Tang Dynasty, and his work influenced many later poets, such as Li Bai, Du Fu and so on.

Enjoy the Poem

Wang Yue Huai Yuan —Looking at the Moon & Missing Someone Far Away was written at the time Zhang Jiuling was demoted. There are 8 lines in this poem. It expresses the feelings of missing a lover or a family member faraway. It is famous because it expresses the feelings of thinking of someone else by the way of imagining how the other is thinking of him, instead of directly describing how the poet misses the other.

Because the first part of the poem is quite famous, it has been included in almost all anthologies of poems. I will also just mainly introduce this part to you.

The first two lines: 海上生明月，天涯共此时 hǎi shàng shēng míng yuè, tiān yá gòng cǐ shí—A bright moon is rising over the sea, we see her from afar at the same time.

The first line catches the "looking at the moon" part of the title, writing about the view, and creating a boundless, gallant and moving view. The second line picks up the second part of the title, "thinking of the person faraway"; the poet writes about the feeling, quickly and totally catching the meaning of the title, that maybe, on the other side of the sea, she is also thinking of him. Instead of speaking for himself, he is thinking of the other person, he says the other person is missing him; the conception is clever and implicative. With such an easy style, he has quickly and totally caught the meaning of the title, which is just one of the characteristics of Zhang's poems—to express his feelings naturally.

The verb "生, shēng" (be in birth, is born, raise) is very vivid, saying the moon "is given birth to" by the sea. The ocean, the moon and the skyline, the poet and the other in his heart on the other side of the ocean in the same moonlight have been connected together, creating a great artistic conception.

Looking at the moon is an act in reality, and to miss someone afar is in the imagination. The first two lines combine the two situations, creating a landscape in the bright moonlight that includes the feeling of thinking of (someone) far away. This leaves plenty of room for the association of ideas and for the imagination.

The third and fourth lines：情人怨遥夜，竟夕起相思 qíng rén yuàn yáo yè, jìng xī qǐ xiāng sī—Sweethearts complain the night is too long, lovesick, we stay up all night.

From the imagination in the second line, coming back to reality, these lines express how the lovers miss each other in the moon-lit night, so that they can't sleep and stay up all night.

The lovers on opposite sides of the ocean think deeply about each other so that they can not sleep, and they do not know when the dawn will come, so that they cannot help "yuàn" —complaining the night is really too long. The word "怨 yuàn" —complain includes so much deep love and unlimited wishes for each other, they look forward to seeing the long night pass, and hope to reach the day when the endless missing of each other during the long nights is over and they are together again.

In the following 4 lines, the poet imagines how his lover (or wife) puts out the candle, puts on some clothes and goes out of the door to look at the moon for a long time, until the dew wets her clothes. Because she can not see him and it is impossible for her to carry a double handful of moonlight to him in the faraway place, she decides to go back to sleep and hopes to see him in a sweet dream.

The deep affection in the poem is expressed serenely, lingeringly and there is not any sorrow; the language is natural and fluent. This style has directly influenced Meng Haoran and Wang Wei in their poetic style.

Inspiration

I enjoy this poem because of its wonderful imagination. I am thinking, if we say that life is the source of art, then, imagination may be the wing of artistic creativity. Without good imagination there would be no great works of art. Anyway, there is positive imagination and negative imagination, and only the former results in positive art works. This will depend on the attitude to life of the artist. Only an artist who has a positive and sincere attitude to life, can have a positive imagination and so create wonderful art works. Do you agree?

With so much enjoyment of this poem, I translated it and wrote a piece of music for the first part in 2006 and created a painting for the poem and the music in 2007. Then at Chinese National Academy of Arts, I painted a painting to go with the music and poem in 2012.

Vocabulary

望月怀远　wàng yuè huái yuǎn　the title of the poem, which means looking at the moon & missing someone afar

望　wàng　*v.*　look over, look up, look at

月　yuè　*n.*　moon

怀　huái　*v.*　think of, miss

远　yuǎn　*adj. / adv.*　afar, far away, distant farness

张九龄　zhāng jiǔ líng　a poet's name in the Tang Dynasty

海上生明月　hǎi shàng shēng míng yuè　A bright moon is rising over the sea.

海　hǎi　*n.*　sea.

上　shàng　*adv.*　over

生　shēng　*v.*　raise, grow up

明　míng　*adj.*　bright

天涯共此时　tiān yá gòng cǐ shí　We see her from afar (in distance) at the same time.

天涯　tiān yá　*n.*　skyline, here it means far away

共　gòng　*v./adv.*　share, together

此时　cǐ shí　at this time, right now

此　cǐ　*pron.*　this

时　shí　*adv.*　when, time

情人怨遥夜　qíng rén yuàn yáo yè　Sweethearts complain the night is too long.

情人　qíng rén　*n.*　lover, sweetheart, sweetie

怨　yuàn　*n./v.*　complain

遥夜　yáo yè　*n.*　long night

遥　yáo　*adj./adv.*　faraway, long

夜　yè　*n.*　night

竟夕起相思　jìng xī qǐ xiāng sī　Lovesick, we stay up all night.

竟夕　jìng xī　whole of a night, all night

竟　jìng　*adj.*　whole

夕　xī　*n.*　night, evening

起　qǐ　*adv.*　stay up

相思　xiāng sī　lovesick

海上生明月，天涯共此时。情人怨遥夜，竟夕起相思。hǎi shàng shēng míng yuè, tiān yá gòng cǐ shí。qíng rén yuàn yáo yè, jìng xī qǐ xiāng sī。

A bright moon is rising over the sea,

we see her from afar at the same time.

Sweethearts complain the night is too long,

Lovesick, we stay up all night.

07. 题都城南庄—Inscription in a Village South of the Capital

题都城南庄—tí dū chéng nán zhuāng

唐—táng　　崔护—cuī hù

去年今日此门中—qù nián jīn rì cǐ mén zhōng,

人面桃花相映红—rén miàn táo huā xiāng yìng hóng。

人面不知何处去—rén miàn bù zhī hé chù qù,

桃花依旧笑春风—táo huā yī jiù xiào chūn fēng。

Inscription in a Village South of the Capital

By Cui Hu　　Tang Dynasty

This day last year at the same gate,

A girl's face and the flowers reflected red with each other.

No one knows where the girl is now,

The peach blossoms are still smiling in the spring breeze.

About the Poet

Cui Hu (time of birth and death unknown) was a poet in Tang Dynasty (618 –907) . He was from Boling (Today's Ding County, Hebei Province). Cui Hu was a successful candidate in the highest imperial examinations in 796, then he became Lingnan Jie Du Shi (Military Governorship) .

He created this poem in his youth, and it became the origin of the love story drama related to Ren Mian Tao Hua—the girl's face and the peach flowers (reflecting each other's glow), in later times.

This story was mainly recorded in the literary sketches Ben Shi Shi, Qinggan by Meng Qi in the Tang Dynasty:

A poet named Cui Hu took a walk in a suburb south of the capital on Tomb-sweeping Day. At a yard gate where peach blossoms were in full bloom, he stopped and asked for a cup of water . A beautiful girl warmly granted his request. They both found each other attractive. On the same day in the following year he went to the same house but the girl was not there. There were only the peach blossoms in the spring breeze. Cui was disappointed and wrote a poem on the left part of the gate.

A few days later he took a casual walk through the same suburb and heard crying from the yard. He knocked on the gate. An old man came out and asked: "Are you Cui Hu?" Cui said "Yes" . The old man cried again and said: "You have killed my daughter. " Cui was surprised and did not know what to say. The old man said: "My daughter has grown up; she is educated and intelligent; she has not got married yet. Since last year, she has often been in a trance and felt disturbed as if having lost something. Recently, I went out with her and when we came back, we found some words on the gate. After reading them she was sick, abstained from food and passed away. I am old and she is my only child. She wanted to find a perfect gentleman to marry and look after me. Now she is dead, did not you kill her?" Then he cried again. Cui was touched and asked if he could also enter the room and cry for her. Then he found her, lying dignifiedly on the bed. Cui rested her head on his leg and said "I am here". Instantly, the girl opened her eyes and became alive again. The old man was very happy and he married his daughter to Cui.

By the good help of his wife, Cui became a successful candidate in the highest imperial examinations and then a good officer.

Since then, the story of "Ren Mian Tao Hua—a girl's face and peach blossoms" has become a typical Chinese Love Story, and has been adapted to many different art works.

Enjoy the Poem

The first two lines: 去年今日此门中，人面桃花相映红 qù nián jīn rì cǐ mén zhōng, rén miàn táo huā xiāng yìng hóng—This day last year at the same gate, a girl's face and flowers reflected red with each other.

These two lines are in retrospect. The first line writes about the time and place, which shows us that this place is deeply remembered in the heart of the poet. The second line writes about the girl, who was among the peach blossoms the previous year. The peach blossoms were already brightly-colored and beautiful in the spring breeze, but the girl's face reflected the peach blossoms with a redder hue. Both of these beautiful things reflected each other, showing us a more wonderful vision and atmosphere.

The last two lines: 人面不知何处去，桃花依旧笑春风 rén miàn bù zhī hé chù qù, táo huā yī jiù xiào chūn fēng—No one knows where the girl is now, the peach blossoms are still smiling in the spring breeze.

At the same place and the same day this year, something is the same and something else is different. The peach blossoms are still there but the girl is not there now. There is only the beautiful memory and a touch of sadness in the heart of the poet.

This little poem is written in a natural style and the poet uses the girl's face and the peach blossoms to link the time he wrote the poem in the same time in the previous year, to compare the similarity and difference. It indirectly expresses the sign of emotion from the bottom of the poet's heart in a lucid and mellow way and there is much aftertaste.

Comparison, reflection and personification are important methods to help the poet to express his feelings in the poem.

Inspiration

When I read the poem, I was smiling together with the peach blossoms. I was glad for the happy outcome of this story and I enjoyed the style of personification in this poem. Since the peach flowers have lives and they are able to smile, birds and the spring can certainly witness this beautiful love story and talk about it to us. Right?

With this idea and a big smile, I translated this poem and created a piece of music for the poem in 2006, and painted a painting to match the music and the poem in 2011. Then I re-painted a new painting as my assignment at Chinese National Academy of Arts to match them in 2012.

Vocabulary

题都城南庄　tí dū chéng nán zhuāng　the title of the poem, which means writing in a village named South Village of the Capital City

题　tí　v./n.　v. inscribe, write　n. title, subject

都城　dū chéng　n.　capital city, here it means Chang'an — today's Xi'an

都　dū　n.　capital, big city

城　chéng　n.　city, town

南　nán　n.　south, southern

庄　zhuāng　n.　village

崔护　cuī hù　a poet's name in the Tang Dynasty

唐　tánɡ　*n.*　the Tang Dynasty（618－907）

去年今日此门中　qù nián jīn rì cǐ mén zhōng　This day last year at the same gate.

去年　qù nián　*n.*　last year

去　qù　*adj.*　past

年　nián　*n.*　year

今日　jīn rì　*n.*　today, this day

今　jīn　*n./pron.*　now, this, today

日　rì　*n.*　sun, day

此　cǐ　*pron.*　this

门　mén　*n.*　gate, door

中　zhōng　*adv.*　in, inside, within

人面桃花相映红　rén miàn táo huā xiāng yìng hóng　A girl's face and the flowers reflected red with each other.

人面　rén miàn　*n.*　face of human being, here it means a beautiful girl, or the face of a beautiful girl

人　rén　*n.*　people, person

面　miàn　*quantifier/n.*　quantifier There is no meaning, to express unit of something flat. *n.*　face, surface

桃花　táo huā　*n.*　peach blossom

桃　táo　*n.*　peach

花　huā　*n.*　flower, blossom

相　xiāng　*adv.*　each other

映　yìng　*v.*　reflect, shine, mirror

红　hóng　*adj.*　red

人面不知何处去　rén miàn bù zhī hé chù qù　No one knows where the girl is now.

不　bù　*adv.*　no, do not

知　zhī　*v.*　know, realize, perceive

何处　hé chù　*adv.*　where

何　　hé　*adv.*　why, where, what, who

处　　chù　*n.*　location, place

桃花依旧笑春风　táo huā yī jiù xiào chūn fēng　The peach blossoms are still smiling in the spring breeze.

依旧　yī jiù　*adv.*　still

笑　　xiào　*v.*　smile, laugh

春风　chūn fēng　*n.*　spring breeze

春　　chūn　*n.*　spring

风　　fēng　*n.*　wind, breeze

去年今日此门中，人面桃花相映红。人面不知何处去，桃花依旧笑春风。qù nián jīn rì cǐ mén zhōng，rén miàn táo huā xiāng yìng hóng。rén miàn bù zhī hé chù qù，táo huā yī jiù xiào chūn fēng。

This day last year at the same gate,

A girl's face and the flowers reflected red with each other.

No one knows where the girl is now,

The peach blossoms are still smiling in the spring breeze.

08. 别董大—A Farewell Song for Dong Da

别董大—bié dǒng dà

唐—táng　高适—gāo shì

千里黄云白日曛—qiān lǐ huáng yún bái rì xūn,

北风吹雁雪纷纷—běi fēng chuī yàn xuě fēn fēn。

莫愁前路无知己—mò chóu qián lù wú zhī jǐ,

天下谁人不识君—tiān xià shuí rén bù shí jūn。

A Farewell Song for Dong Da

By Gao Shi　Tang Dynasty

Yellow clouds stretch for a thousand miles, covering the sunlight.

The north wind blows the wild geese through the flurrying snow.

Don't worry there is no dear friend on the road（ahead）.

In the world there is no one who doesn't know you.

About the Poet

Gao Shi 高适 gāo shì (700 – 765) was from Hebei Province and was an important representative of Frontier Fortress Poetry in the Tang Dynasty (618 – 907).

The most flourishing times of Tang Poetry was in the Glorious Age of Tang Dynasty. Besides Li Bai and Du Fu, there were many other great poets during that period. Some of these poets and their works can be summarized into two big genres. One is the Landscape, Field and Garden Poetry genre, Wang Wei and Meng Haoran being their representative poets; the other is the Frontier Fortress Poetry genre, Gao Shi and Cen Shen being their representative poets.

In the Glorious Age of Tang Dynasty, the frontier was very long; there were many garrison troops, and there were many opportunities for the poets to work in the frontier regions. Therefore, many of them wished to join the army to pursue their careers. With this background, they created many poems that described the landscape of the border areas, recorded their army lives, and their dreams of working for the country; they expressed the feelings of the soldiers in the frontier fortress. In this genre, apart from Gao Shi and Cen Shen, there were also Wang Changling, Li Qi, Wang Zhihuan and Wang Han and many other poets. As the representative poets of the genre, Gao Shi and Cen Shen are also known collectively as Gao and Cen.

Gao Shi was born into a quite poor family in Bohai Tiao Xian (Today's Jing County, or the other version: Cang County, Hebei Province), and was a beggar in his teenage years. When he was about 20 years old, he went to the capital—Chang'an (Today's Xi'an) to find his way, but returned disappointedly. In his middle age, he wandered or drifted through Liang, Song, Yan, Zhao (today's Henan and Hebei Provinces), until he was nearly 50 years old. By the recommendation of

Zhang Jiugao, he was appointed to be a Fengqiu Xianwei (An official just below the head of a county). In this position, he felt "拜迎长官心欲碎, 鞭挞黎庶令人悲" bài yíng zhǎng guān xīn yù suì, biān tà lí shù lìng rén bēi —My heart was broken when I had to pay homage to some bad senior officers; my heart was sad when I saw them lash the ordinary people). Therefore, he left this position and became a military staff officer of Ge Shuhan who was Hexi Jie Du Shi (a military governor of Hexi). During the Rebellion of An and Shi (755 – 763), Ge Shuhan was defeated and lost Tongguan. The emperor Xuan Zong had to escape from the capital. Gao Shi caught up with Xuan Zong and told him about the battle in Tongguan. He was then appointed to be a Shi Yushi (Imperial Clerk). After that his official rank rose higher and higher, to the position of Jie Du Shi (Military Governorship), in charge of both civil and military work in several provinces several times until he became the Marquis of Bohai Tiao Xian.

The representative works of Gao Shi were his frontier-style poems and the poems that reflected the people's lives. With a positive attitude to life, heroic spirit, an exoteric but refreshing language and a euphemistic and flowing melody, he expressed the magnificent scenery of the frontier and the real lives of the soldiers.

Enjoy the Poem

Bie Dong Da—A Farewell Song for Dong Da is a little poem, expressing Gao Shi's feeling on sending off his friend Dong Da.

Dong Da was the name of a famous musician Dong Lanting in the Tang Dynasty. Dong was his family name, Da means old, meaning he was the eldest one among his brothers, so he was called Dong Da.

Dong Da was a famous master of the musical instrument—Qi Xian Qin (Heptachord). In the Glorious Age of Tang Dynasty, there were many cultural exchanges among the Han People and the other nationalities. The music of non-Han nationalities was quite popular, but few musicians understood how to play Qi Xian Qin—heptachord. However, Dong Da was one of the master musicians who could play it expertly.

This poem was written in Suiyang (in today's Henan Province) in 747. At that time, the poet Gao Shi and his friend Dong Da met each other after being apart for a long time. After a short reunion, they would have to part again.

The first two lines：千里黄云白日曛，北风吹雁雪纷纷 qiān lǐ huáng yún bái rì xūn, běi fēng chuī yàn xuě fēn fēn—Yellow clouds stretch for a thousand miles, covering the sunlight. The north wind blows the wild geese through the flurrying snow.

With the simplest words, the two lines describe the time and environment in which they parted. On the surface, it is writing about the landscape, but reading between the lines, we can hear the sound of the wind, see the birds in the heavy snow and feel the spirit of the heroes on the peaks of the mountains.

It was just in this sort of desolate, cold and vast environment that the poet Gao Shi was about to send off his friend, who had a unique musical skill but had not been recognized yet.

Instead of doing what most of people do when they have to say goodbye with a sad feeling, in this poem Gao Shi spoke his parting words of advice with quite a positive emotion and encouraging style.

The last two lines：莫愁前路无知己，天下谁人不识君 mò chóu qián lù wú zhī jǐ, tiān xià shuí rén bù shí jūn—Don't worry there is no dear friend on the road (ahead). In the world there is no one who doesn't know you.

With a very positive attitude to life, and very resonant and strong sounds, he encouraged his friend to make the effort to pursue his dream with much more confidence and strength. These two lines bring a warm feeling to his friend in the cold winter.

Since Dong Da—Dong Lanting was a highly accomplished player of string instruments, he would certainly meet someone who could understand him on the road ahead.

Because they were close friends, they could speak in a simple, unrestrained and frank manner, and although they were both in a frustrating situation at that time, they could take comfort in their hope for the future.

The last two lines are very optimistic and bring to the whole of the little poem a heroic feeling; there is no sorrowful feeling at all.

Inspiration

This is one of my favorite farewell poems. I love it because of the positive life attitude inside, and the deep caring for a close friend. When I asked myself why the short 4 lines could touch people so much, two lines from a lyric by Qin Guan in Song Dynasty jumped into my mind: "两情若是久长时，又岂在朝朝暮暮 liǎng qíng ruò shì jiǔ cháng shí，yòu qǐ zài zhāo zhāo mù mù—If love between both sides can last forever, why do they need to stay together night and day? " It talks about love, and I think it can express a similar situation between friends. When a precious friendship and feeling can be kept forever in two hearts, why must they always stay together?

Being moved so much, I translated this poem and wrote a piece of music for it in 2005, created a painting for them in 2010, and then I painted a new painting as my assignment at Chinese National Academy in 2012.

Vocabulary

别董大　　bié dǒng dà　　the title of the poem, which means a farewell song for Dong Da

别　bié　v.　seeing-off

董大　dǒng dà　*n.*　Dong Da—a musician who was famous for playing the Qi Xian Qin (heptachord) in the Tang Dynasty. His real name was Dong Lanting (董兰庭). He was a good friend of the poet. Because he was the eldest among his brothers, he was called Dong Da (董大). Dong is his family name. (In Chinese, the naming order is family name first with given name afterwards.)

高适　gāo shì　a poet's name in the Tang Dynasty

千里黄云白日曛　qiān lǐ huáng yún bái rì xūn　Yellow clouds stretch for a thousand miles, covering the sunlight.

千　qiān　*quantifier*　thousand

里　lǐ　*quantifier*　a Chinese unit of length (= 1/2 kilometer) here, we can understand it as "mile"

黄　huáng　*adj. / n.*　*adj.*　yellow　*n.*　a Chinese family name

云　yún　*n.*　cloud

白日　bái rì　*n.*　sun, sunlight

白　bái　*adj.*　white

日　rì　*n.*　sun, day

曛　xūn　*adj.*　dusky

北风吹雁雪纷纷　běi fēng chuī yàn xuě fēn fēn　The north wind blows the wild geese through the flurrying of snow.

北　běi　*n.*　north, northern

风　fēng　*n.*　wind, breeze

吹　chuī　*v.*　blow

雁　yàn　*n.*　wild goose

雪　xuě　*n.*　snow

纷纷　fēn fēn　*phrase*　one after another, in succession

莫愁前路无知己　mò chóu qián lù wú zhī jǐ　Don't worry there is no dear / bosom friend on the road ahead.

莫　mò　*adv.*　no, don't

愁　chóu　*v.*　worry, be anxious of

前   qián   *adj.*   ahead, in front of

路   lù   *n.*   road, way

无   wú   *v.*   there is no, not have

知己   zhī jǐ   *n.*   bosom friend

天下谁人不识君   tiān xià shuí rén bù shí jūn   In the world, there is no one who doesn't know you.

天下   tiān xià   *n.*   under the sun, whole of China under heaven, all over the world, between heaven and earth, everything under heaven

谁人   shuí rén   *n.*   who

谁   shuí   *n.*   who, whom

人   rén   *n.*   people, person

不   bù   *adv.*   no, do not

识   shí   *v.*   know, recognize

君   jūn   *n.*   gentleman, here it refers to Dong Da

千里黄云白日曛，北风吹雁雪纷纷。莫愁前路无知己，天下谁人不识君。qiān lǐ huáng yún bái rì xūn, běi fēng chuī yàn xuě fēn fēn。mò chóu qián lù wú zhī jǐ, tiān xià shuí rén bù shí jūn。

Yellow clouds stretch for a thousand miles, covering the sunlight.

The north wind blows the wild geese through the flurrying snow.

Don't worry there is no dear friend on the road (ahead).

In the world there is no one who doesn't know you.

09. 赋得古原草送别—Send off on the Ancient Plain（The First Part）

赋得古原草送别（第一部分）—fù dé gǔ yuán cǎo sòng bié

唐—táng　白居易—bái jū yì

离离原上草—lí lí yuán shàng cǎo,

一岁一枯荣—yī suì yī kū róng。

野火烧不尽—yě huǒ shāo bú jìn,

春风吹又生—chūn fēng chuī yòu shēng。

Send Off on the Ancient Plain（The First Part）

By Bai Juyi　Tang Dynasty

Lush grass grows on the ancient plain,

Each year it withers and flourishes.

Wild fire can't burn it out,

It re-grows in the spring breeze.

About the Poet

Bai Juyi 白居易 bái jū yì（772 – 846）was one of the greatest poets in the Tang Dynasty（618 – 907）. His ancestral home was in Taiyuan, Shanxi, then moved to Xiagui（in today's Shangxi）. He was born in Henan.

Bai Juyi lived in the chaotic period caused by the wars of the Tang Dynasty military governors, experienced 6 emperors from Dezong to Wenzong and lived in a family that was scholarly but poor. This helped him to understand more about real society and life of the common people.

In 799, when he was 27 years old, he became a successful candidate in the highest imperial examinations. He was then appointed as an official in various positions.

He was demoted in 815 for daring to speak out the truth and this offended his superiors. In the position as Jiangzhou Si Ma（an assistant to the Ci Shi—feudal provincial or prefectural governor, which wasn't a position that could work for the country, but a place to be offered to the officers who were demoted）, he saw how the ordinary people lived, which helped him write many realistic poems and become one of the greatest poets in the Tang Dynasty after Li Bai and Du Fu.

He was then appointed as a feudal provincial or prefectural governor in Zhongzhou, Hangzhou and Suzhou, then to some higher positions, such as the teacher of the crown prince and a minister in the Ministry of Justice.

After he retired, he stayed in Luoyang. He died in 846, at the age of 75.

Bai Juyi mainly followed Confucianism, while also accepted Taoism and Buddhism. His guiding principle in life was the idea "达则兼济天下，穷则独善其身"（dá zé jiān jì tiān xià, qióng zé dú shàn qí shēn—If I am successful, I will help this world with my ability and wealth; if I am poor, limited and unsuccessful, I will keep my own personal virtues）. Therefore, in the mind of Bai Juyi, there was the very positive hand of

Confucianism, in which he wanted to have a successful career; on the other hand, he was affected by Taoism and Buddhism. Generally, when he was young, he was quite positive and wanted to help this world; when he became older, especially when he was demoted, he mainly wanted to keep his own clean and personal virtues. In his later years, the ideas of Taoism and Buddhism were his main guiding thoughts. All of these thoughts and changes were reflected in his poetry.

In literature, Bai Juyi summarized the theory of realism from *Shi Jing* (*Book of Poetry*), *Han Yue Fu* (*Folk Poetry and Music in the Han Dynasty*) and Du Fu, outlined a clear-cut theory of poetry and literary opinion. He mainly thought that "文章合为时而著，歌诗合为事而发" [wén zhāng hé wèi shí ér zhù, gē shī hé wèi shì ér fā—Articles should be written for the times, and poetry (and music, as then the poems could be sung) should be written about meaningful things]. This would require writers and poets to care about the times they lived in and to do something positive for the times and for society. It became the theoretical basis of the Movement of New Yue Fu (Movement of New Folk Music and Poetry in the Tang Dynasty).

In poetry creation, Bai Juyi sorted his own poems into four types:

Feng Yu Shi: Allegorical Poems—with implicit words to criticize or advise someone or something, mainly reflecting on national affairs or civilian lives, he cared about politics and spoke for people; there was a strong sense of justice and responsibility in this kind of poems.

Xian Shi Shi: Poems of Leisure.

Gan Shang Shi: Sentimental Poems.

Za lv: Poems with various themes.

Among these categories, Bai Juyi paid most attention to his Feng Yu Poetry and thought this kind of poetry expressed his "兼济之志" (jiān jì zhī zhì—desire to help the world with his ability and wisdom).

The main character of Bai Juyi's poetry is in a realistic style. He caught some significant subjects, reflected on important historic events, revealed social contradictions, and made his poems reflect a wide social life; with his bright artistic methods, he revealed many features of the people in his times and reflected their thoughts and lives. By using folk language in his poetry, the words are simple but the meanings are deep, and this makes his poems bright, pure and natural, and his poems are welcomed by common people.

By the good lead and influence of Bai Juyi, the Movement of New Yue Fu was developed to a new level. Bai Juyi's poetry was the peak of poetic realism in its time.

Bai Juyi left more than 2,800 poems to the world and many of them are very long.

Enjoy the Poem

This poem was written in 787. The two words "Fu de" in the title show us that it was an assignment that the poet wrote to prepare for the examination in accordance with the rules of the national imperial examination in the Tang Dynasty. There are some very strict rules for writing this kind of poetry, so there are not many good works of this kind; however, this poem has been on everybody's lips for more than 1,200 years.

This poem was written when Bai Juyi was 16. That year, he went to the capital—Chang'an. With his poems, he paid a formal visit to Gu Kuang.

At first, Gu Kuang made a joke with the name of Bai Juyi ("Ju Yi" in Chinese means "it is easy to live somewhere") and said that rice was expensive in Chang'an, so it was not easy to live there at all. But when he read the words "yě huǒ shāo bú jìn, chūn fēng chuī yòu shēng", he could not help being greatly appreciative: If he was able to write such wonderful poetry, "Ju Yi —it will be easy to live anywhere". And then, because of Gu Kuang's recommendation, quickly, Bai Juyi's reputation was greatly boosted.

There are eight lines in this poem, but in common with most people, I will only introduce the first four.

The first two line：离离原上草，一岁一枯荣 lí lí yuán shàng cǎo, yī suì yī kū róng—Lush grass grows on the ancient plain, each year it withers and flourishes.

The first line explains the essence of the title with the words "ancient", "plain" and "grass"：What lush grass covers the ancient plain! They are very ordinary words, but they capture one of the characteristics of the grass—its exuberant vitality.

The second line introduces another characteristic of the grass—each year it withers and flourishes. When I translated it, I thought for a long time and I asked myself whether I should translate it as "each year it flourishes and then withers" in accordance with the natural life cycle of the grass. Then, I decided to stick closely to the original because "it flourishes and then withers", writes about the grass in the autumn whereas "it withers and flourishes", writes about the grass in the spring.

This line not only describes the natural life cycle of the grass, but also acts as a preparation for the next line.

The last two lines：野火烧不尽，春风吹又生 yě huǒ shāo bù jìn, chūn fēng chuī yòu shēng—Wild fire can not burn it out, it re-grows in the spring breeze.

The two famous lines develop the words "withers" and "flourishes", and further describe the most important characteristic of the grass, its strong life force, meanwhile "painting" two beautiful pictures. It can not be burnt out completely; it can not be uprooted at all. With the lines "wild fire can not burn it out", the poet creates a more heroic artistic conception.

Wild fire is strong and terrible. It can destroy everything and can burn the grass in the twinkling of an eye. However, no matter how strong the fire is, it can not burn out the roots of the grass. As soon as the spring breeze blows across the ancient plain, it will reawaken, re-grow and rocover the ground quickly.

By emphasizing the power of the wild fire the author also emphasizes the power of the grass to re-grow in spring.

The hot and red wild fire is strong; but the soft and green grass is stronger. The fourth line echoes the first line; but not only does it express the character of the grass once more, it also expresses an idea of the poet —a thing of beauty cannot be destroyed forever, it will usually re-emerge in the right conditions.

When I wrote this, I could not help thinking of the story of the Rise of the Phoenix. They have different approaches but both of them have an equally satisfactory outcome.

This poem uses very simple language and is neat and orderly; every word is exact and meaningful. It has become well liked by Chinese people and the third and fourth lines have become very famous since they were first written.

Inspiration

Anything just or beautiful cannot be suppressed forever, even though it is suppressed temporarily. When the time is suitable, it will re-emerge, just like the grass on the plain; it is burnt out in autumn but sure to re-grow up in the next spring. Do you agree with me?

With so much appreciation for the little grass, I translated this poem and wrote a piece of music for it in 2006, created a painting to go with them in 2010. Then I painted a new painting as my assignment at Chinese National Academy of Arts in 2012.

Vocabulary

赋得古原草送别　　fù dé gǔ yuán cǎo sòng bié　　the title of the

poem meaning sending off on the ancient plain

赋得　　fù dé　　to write a poem according to an appointed title

In ancient China, when a poet wrote a poem to a given title, he had to add these two words. This poem was a practice poem that the poet wrote to prepare for his examination in the capital before starting his official career, so, he added the two words. Here there is no other meaning.

古　　gǔ　*adj.*　ancient, old

原　　yuán　*adv.*　plain

草　　cǎo　*n.*　grass

送别　　sòng bié　*v.*　send off

白居易　　bái jū yì　a poet's name in the Tang Dynasty

唐　　táng　*n.*　the Tang Dynasty (618 – 907)

离离原上草　　lí lí yuán shàng cǎo　Luxuriant/Lush grass grows on the ancient plain.

离离　　lí lí　*adj.*　lush, luxuriant, thick

上　　shàng　*adv.*　over, on

一岁一枯荣　　yī suì yī kū róng　Each year it withers and flourishes.

一　　yī　*numeral*　one, a

岁　　suì　*n.*　year

枯　　kū　*v. /adj.*　wither, withered

荣　　róng　*v. /adj.*　flourish, grow luxuriantly

野火烧不尽　　yě huǒ shāo bù jìn　Wild fire cannot burn it out.

野火　　yě huǒ　*n.*　wild fire

野　　yě　*adj.*　wild

火　　huǒ　*n.*　fire

烧　　shāo　*v.*　burn

不　　bù　*adv.*　no, do not

尽　　jìn　*v. /adj.*　end, all, complete

春风吹又生　　chūn fēng chuī yòu shēng　It re-grows in the spring breeze.

春风　　chūn fēng　*n.*　spring breeze

春　　chūn　*n.*　spring

风　　fēng　*n.*　wind, breeze

吹　　chuī　*v.*　blow

又　　yòu　*adv.*　again

生　　shēng　*v.*　raise, grow up

离离原上草，一岁一枯荣。野火烧不尽，春风吹又生。lí lí yuán shàng cǎo, yī suì yī kū róng。 yě huǒ shāo bù jìn, chūn fēng chuī yòu shēng。

Lush grass grows on the ancient plain,

Each year it withers and flourishes.

Wild fire can't burn it out,

It re-grows in the spring breeze.

10. 山中问答—Question and Answer on the Mountain

山中问答—shān zhōng wèn dá

　　唐—táng　李白— lǐ bái

问余何意栖碧山—wèn yú hé yì qī bì shān,

笑而不答心自闲—xiào ér bù dá xīn zì xián。

桃花流水杳然去—táo huā liú shuǐ yǎo rán qù,

别有天地非人间—bié yǒu tiān dì fēi rén jiān。

Question and Answer on the Mountain

　　By Li Bai　Tang Dynasty

People ask me why I dwell on the Green Mountain,

I respond with a smile, my heart is at leisure.

Peach blossoms in the water flow far away,

There is another wonderland beyond the human world.

About the Poet

Li Bai 李白 lǐ bái（701 – 762）is one of the greatest, the most renowned and admired poets in China. The land of his ancestors was Chengji, Longxi（today's Qinan, Gansu Province）. At the end of the Sui Dynasty（581 – 618）, his forefathers went to Cuiye［part of Anxi Duhufu during the Tang Dynasty（618 – 907）, today's Kyrgyzstan］and that was the place of Li Bai's birth. When he was very young, about 5 years old, he moved to Changlong, Mianzhou（today's Jiangyou, Sichuan）with his father.

Li Bai was influenced by both Confucianism and Taoism. He started to travel around the country when he was 25 years old. He then entered the imperial court and became a member of the Han-lin Academy at the age of 42. He was greatly delighted and eager to serve the emperor as a capable statesman. However, the Emperor Xuanzong only used him as a wonderful palace poet to write trivial lyrics. He was unwilling to serve as such a meaningless function, so he left the capital after less than two years and started his second period of travel, aimlessly wandering all over the country. He was then charged with being an adherent of the rebel cause and sentenced to exile, though he was pardoned while on the way. He died of an illness at Dangtu in today's Anhui.

Li Bai lived during the most flourishing times in Tang Dynasty. Most of his poems reflected the positive spirit of the times. He is considered to be the foremost romantic poet of the Tang Dynasty and his writing style has influenced poets down to the present time.

More than 1,000 poems wrote by Li Bai are still in existence. They are very popular and are recited by the Chinese from their childhood.

Enjoy the Poem

This is a seven-character quatrain (each line consists of seven characters, and has a strict tonal pattern and rhyming scheme) with a light and faraway poetic flavor. It expresses the poet's leisurely and peaceful heart, caring little for fame and gain and detaches from secular society, and it also expresses his fondness for nature.

For a period of time, Li Bai idled on Bi (Green) Mountain. Someone wondered why he lived on the mountain and he wrote this poem as an answer. Another title of the poem is *Shan Zhong Da Su Ren* — *Answer to the Layfolk from the Mountain* .

Bi Mountain is in today's Anlu county, Hubei Province. According to the records of Anlu County annals, another name for Baizhao Mountain is Bi Mountain. On the mountain there is "peach blossom rock", it is said that this is just the place where Li Bai used to read his books.

The first line: 问余何意栖碧山 wèn yú hé yì qī bì shān —People ask me why I dwell on the Green Mountain.

Since the other title of the poem is *Answer to the Layfolk (common people) from the Mountain* , this line implies the person who asks the question is someone common; the question highlights the subject of the poem and captures our attention. Bi Mountain is the name of the mountain, Bi, means "green", and hints that the environment is peaceful and beautiful.

Anyway, when the questioner wants to hear the answer, the poet intentionally does not answer.

The second line: 笑而不答心自闲 xiào ér bù dá xīn zì xián—I respond with a smile, my heart is at leisure.

"xīn zì xián—my heart is easy and at leisure" not only reflects poet's heart when he is on the mountain, but also points out that the question in the first line is not something new, "Something I know already, however,

I just do not want to tell you because something wonderful is difficult to express in words. "

Therefore, I smile to your question, but do not answer, just let you guess. This keeps the reader in suspense, while adding change and making the poem absorbing. The emotion and attitude to life of the poet are expressed through the word "xian—peaceful, leisurely and easy".

The last two lines: 桃花流水杳然去，别有天地非人间 táo huā liú shuǐ yǎo rán qù, bié yǒu tiān dì fēi rén jiān—Peach blossoms in the water flow far way, there is another wonderland beyond the human world.

While in these two lines the author writes about the landscape of the Green Mountain, which is in fact answering the question in a skillful way, telling people why he lives in the mountain and hinting at his good emotional state at that time.

Let us imagine: on a spring day, by a small streamlet that flows through the forest, the sight of pink peach blossoms accompanying the green mountains, together the fallen petals flow far away with the water; a poet is sitting on the huge stone reading a book. Isn't that just like "Shi Wai Tao Yuan—Arcadia"?

These two lines combine the peaceful environment and the easy heart of the poet. It does not have an answer, but also there is an answer already. They write about the landscape in the late spring, but, there is not any sadness as there is with many poems that express how people do not have the ability to hang on to the spring.

The last line: bié yǒu tiān dì fēi rén jiān—There is another wonderland beyond the human world. It states the poet's feelings frankly. On the peaceful mountain, there is another distinctive wonderland, which is beyond the world of human beings and is much better than the hustle and bustle of human society. Here is just the best outcome; it is his ideal Spiritual Home. This is to answer with a non-answer.

Now we have seen that there are only 4 lines in this little poem, but there are many things in it: question, answer, statement, depiction and remark; much content is contained within a short space and with a natural and simple language, a leisurely and easy tone, deep connotation and a light and faraway artistic conception.

If we think of the fate of Li Bai, we can understand why he would have liked staying on the Green Mountain, "ān néng cuī méi zhé yāo shì quán guì, shǐ wǒ bù dé kāi xīn yán—How can I bow down to the nobility if that puts me in a state of unhappiness?" (the last line of*Meng You Tian Mu Yin Liu Bie* by Li Bai)

Since his dream could not come true in reality, since he loved freedom and was innocent and romantic, the best method for him to detach himself from the heavy and cruel reality was to go into the natural world of the mountains and water. Only when he was there, would his talent and passion be really developed and released and his soul be at peace forever.

The famous politician, calligrapher and poet Li Dongyuan (1447 – 1556) in Ming Dynasty (1368 – 1644) said: "The value of a poem depends on its meaning. The value of the meaning depends on its distance, not its nearness, its lightness not its thickness; something thick and near can be seen clearly; something light and faraway is difficult to know. For example ... Li Tai Bai's 'táo huā liú shuǐ yǎo rán qù, bié yǒu tiān dì fēi rén jiān' —peach blossoms in the water flow far away; there is another wonderland beyond the human world...something light but strong, near but faraway, it is difficult to explain to the common people."

Inspiration

I enjoy Li Bai's poems, not only for their wonderful artistic conception, but also because I like his liberal attitude to life. After all, in this world, besides being an officer to work for the country, there are many more roads on which we can go, and many more things we can do, to enjoy ourselves and to help this world. Therefore, we should not keep going on just one road and if we have realized it is not the road most suitable for us, the cleverest way is to give it up, to open up or to go on a new road, and to enjoy another landscape. The sooner we give up on something that is not going to be successful, the better. Do you agree?

With much appreciation for Li Bai, I translated this poem and created a piece of music for it in 2007, and then I painted a painting to go with it as my assignment at Chinese National Academy of Arts in 2012.

Vocabulary

山中问答　shān zhōng wèn dá　the title of the poem which means question and answer on the mountain

山　shān　*n.*　mountain, hill

中　zhōng　*adv.*　in, inside, within

问　wèn　*v.*　ask, question

答　dá　*v.*　answer, reply

李白　lǐ bái　a poet's name in the Tang Dynasty

唐　táng　*n.*　the Tang Dynasty（618 – 907）

问余何意栖碧山　wèn yú hé yì qī bì shān　People ask me why I dwell on the Green Mountain.

余　yú　*n.*　I, me

何　hé　*adv.*　why, where, what, who, here means why

意　yì　*n./v.*　*n.* meaning, here it means "feeling"　*v.* mean, here it means "feel"

栖　qī　*v.*　dwell, perch, stay

碧　bì　*adj.*　bluish green, green

山　shān　*n.*　mountain, hill

碧山　bì shān　*n.*　Green Mountain or Bi Mountain; name of a mountain, in today's Anlu County, Hubei Province

笑而不答心自闲　xiào ér bù dá xīn zì xián　I respond with a

smile, my heart is at leisure.

笑　xiào　*v.*　smile, laugh

而　ér　*conj.*　but

不　bù　*adv.*　no, not

心　xīn　*n.*　heart, mind, feeling

自　zì　*adj.*　oneself, self , here it means comfortable, at ease

闲　xián　*adj.*　easy, carefree, at leisure

桃花流水杳然去　táo huā liú shuǐ yǎo rán qù　Peach blossoms in the water flow far away.

桃花　táo huā　*n.*　peach blossom,

流水　liú shuǐ　*n.*　running water, stream

杳　yǎo　*adj.*　distant and out of sight

然　rán　*adj. / adv.*　the suffix of an adjective or adverb, to help to express the meaning "look like"

杳然　yǎo rán　*adv.*　far away, without a trace

去　qù　*v.*　go, leave, here means "flow"

别有天地非人间　bié yǒu tiān dì fēi rén jiān　There is another wonderland (heaven and earth) beyond the human world.

别　bié　*v.*　the other, another

有　yǒu　*v.*　there is / are, have

天地　tiān dì　heaven and earth; world; universe, here it means a "wonderland"

天　tiān　*n.*　sky, heaven

地　dì　*n.*　the earth, land

非　fēi　*adv.*　not

人间　rén jiān　*n.*　human world

问余何意栖碧山，笑而不答心自闲。桃花流水杳然去，别有天地非人间。wèn yú hé yì qī bì shān, xiào ér bù dá xīn zì xián. táo huā liú shuǐ yǎo rán qù, bié yǒu tiān dì fēi rén jiān。

People ask me why I dwell on the Green Mountain,

I respond with a smile, my heart is at leisure.

Peach blossoms in the water flow far away,

There is another wonderland beyond the human world.

11. 早梅—The Plum Blossoms in the Early Spring

早梅—zǎo méi

唐—táng　张谓—zhāng wèi

一树寒梅白玉条—yī shù hán méi bái yù tiáo，

迥临村路傍溪桥—jiǒng lín cūn lù bàng xī qiáo。

不知近水花先发—bù zhī jìn shuǐ huā xiān fā，

疑是经冬雪未消—yí shì jīng dōng xuě wèi xiāo。

The Plum Blossoms in the Early Spring

By Zhang Wei　Tang Dynasty

Flowers cover a plum blossom tree like the white jade in the cold,

Far away from the village road and near the bridge over the stream.

I didn't know the flowers by the water would blossom earlier.

I thought it was the winter snow had not melted yet.

About the Poet

Zhang Wei 张谓 zhāng wèi（? – 777）was from Henei, today's Biyang County, Henan Province. He earned his Jin Shi title（the successful candidate of the highest imperial examinations）in 743. He had served in the military for more than 10 years before being appointed to official positions, like Shang Shu Lang（尚书郎）, Ci Shi（刺史）（provincial or prefectural governor）of Tan Zhou and then Li Bu Shi Lang（礼部侍郎）.

The characteristics of his poems are refined wording, depth of meaning and clear poetic style. *Zao Mei —The Plum Blossoms in the Early Spring* is one of his representative works and has been included in almost all Chinese classical poetry collections.

The Symbolized Meaning of Plum Blossoms

In Chinese culture, the Plum Blossom symbolizes:

Gu Qi（骨气）—strength of character, moral integrity and backbone;

Gang Yi（刚毅）—fortitude, indefatigability, perseverance and tenacity;

Xing Fu and Ji Xiang（幸福吉祥）—bless, luck and propitiousness.

According to Confucianism, the plum blossom is the symbol of a gentleman who has nobility, personal integrity, fortitude and the heroic quality that do not retreat from adversity. In modern China, Mr. Mao Zedong's lyric *Yong Mei—Ode to the Plum Blossom* endowed the plum blossom with some of the spirit of the times, such as clean breath, steadfastness in the cold season, faithfulness, constancy, firmness, independence and self-reliance. Mr. Mao emphasized that these qualities were in fact the root of the Chinese national verve.

The plum blossom is also the symbol of happiness and luck.

The ancient Chinese believed that plum had four virtues: "初生为元，开花如亨，结子为利，成熟为贞。(chū shēng wéi yuán, kāi huā rú hēng, jié zǐ wéi lì, chēng shú wéi zhēn。)" —When it buds, it means everything will be reborn and a new year will start; when it blossoms, it means there will be prosperity and things will go smoothly; when it seeds, it means that there will be benefit everywhere; when it matures, it means constancy (another version: satisfaction for the whole of one's life).

The four words "元，亨，利，贞 (yuán, hēng, lì and zhēn)" — beginning, smoothness, benefit and constancy/satisfaction—are the general symbols of *Yi Jing—The Book of Changes*.

In the Song Dynasty (960 – 1279), it was thought that these four words expressed four phases of things from their beginnings through their development to maturity, which was called "贞下起元 (zhēn xià qǐ yuán)". This phrase then became one of the terms of ancient Chinese philosophy to express the process by which things go from their beginnings to maturity.

There is another idiom in folk tradition "梅开五福 (méi kāi wǔ fú)", meaning the plum blossom has five petals which respectively symbolize delight, happiness, longevity, smoothness and peace.

In folk art, you can often see a picture of a pied magpie on a plum blossom which means:

"喜报早春 (xǐ bào zǎo chūn)" —the pied magpie is reporting that the spring has come early;

"喜报春光 (xǐ bào chūn guāng)" —the pied magpie is reporting that the spring has come;

"喜上眉梢 (xǐ shàng méi shāo)" —happiness appears on the eyebrows, the phrase using the same pronunciation of xǐ què (pied magpie) and xǐ shì (something happy, delightful and lucky), and méi (plum blossom) and méi (eyebrows) to express the meaning.

Enjoy the Poem

Since the ancient time, the plum blossom has been praised by numerous poets in China; some praised its features, some praised its verve, and this poem emphasizes the word "早（zǎo）" —early.

In early spring, before the snow has completely melted, no other flowers have blossomed and there is only the plum blossom bringing vitality and life to the world.

The first line: 一树寒梅白玉条 yī shù hán méi bái yù tiáo—Flowers cover a plum blossom tree like the white jade in the cold.

This line introduces the time that the plum tree blossoms and the features of it: the whole of the tree is covered with thick and numerous flowers and looks like white jade in the early spring. It blossoms early (zǎo, 早), so the flowers have to grow in the cold (hán, 寒) season. By emphasizing the visible and charming features of the plum blossom, this line hints at the characteristics of the plum blossom—strong mind, bravery, having the ability to survive in adversity.

The second line: 迥临村路傍溪桥 jiǒng lín cūn lù bàng xī qiáo— Far away from the village road and near the bridge over the stream.

This line describes the environment where the plum grows. Although a tree has no way of choosing where it grows, this line endows the early plum blossom with human thoughts and ideas, as if the plum tree intentionally grows and blossoms far away from the village road and lives in a remote place, near the water and by the stream. Just like some excellent people, it does not pursue earthliness and does not play to the crowd.

Following the first line, the second line creates a wider artistic conception for the poem. It is a link between the previous and following lines.

The third line: 不知近水花先发 bù zhī jìn shuǐ huā xiān fā—I did not know the flowers by the water would blossom earlier.

This line tells us why this particular plum (blossom) tree blossoms earlier. Because it is growing by the water.

The last line: 疑是经冬雪未消 yí shì jīng dōng xuě wèi xiāo—I thought it was the winter snow that had not melted yet.

The last line recalls the first line. Because it blossoms "早" —early, when the snow has not completely melted, it gives the poet an illusion and he mistakes the white plum blossoms for white snow that has not yet melted in the early spring.

The words "不知（bù zhī）" —don't know—and "疑（yí）" —suspect, describe how the poet felt hazy and in a trance when he saw the plum (blossom) tree from far away, and then when he went nearer and looked at it carefully, he found it was just a tree of plum blossoms that, near the water, had blossomed early. Now the doubt has melted and the word "early" in the title has been echoed.

The "flowers as if snow" in the last line echoes the "plum blossom as white jade" in the first line; it indirectly carries on the connotation of the poem and the theme becomes deeper.

After inheriting and extending the writing of the first two lines, the last two lines express the poet's feelings of surprise.

There are thousands of poems that praise the plum blossom in Chinese poetry. Zhang Wei's *Zao Mei* stands there peacefully and gracefully, just like a girl in a white dress who does not wear makeup. When we see it from far away, it hides among the numerous beauties, and when we look at it from nearby, we can feel how light, elegant, clean and wonderful it is, with a leisurely and artistic conception. How did the poet achieve this?

He uses some simple, easy, refined and frank words by capturing something special about the reality of life and expresses the main meaning of the poem and the poet's love for the plum blossom. For example:

the color of the early plum blossom: white as jade, clean and noble;

the place it grows: far away from the village road and near the bridge over the stream—not pursuing earthliness;

the season it blossoms: in the early spring—it can stand the cold weather and live in harsh conditions;

its features: beautiful, pure, clean and noble.

The poet also used an illusion that binds the plum blossom and snow together—from the feeling of plum blossom like white jade and taking it as the winter snow, to knowing it was just the clean white plum blossom—to describe the whole process by which he had seen, thought and explored. We can not only enjoy a series of vivid views and appreciate the charming plum blossom, but also feel the never-failing meanings in the poem.

Inspiration

Apart from all of the good characters of the plum blossom already have been mentioned, what I admire most are the qualities that Mr. Mao Zedong has pointed out in his famous lyric:

Never vying with the spring for its beauty,

Just being the messenger of the spring.

When the mountain flowers are in full bloom,

She will smile among the flowers.

Plum flower can blossom in the ice and snow in early spring; however, instead of being proud of itself, it keeps a modest and unobtrusive attitude, not envying anyone else which is more beautiful than it, just keep smiling among all sorts of flowers when they are in full bloom. Just like those great pioneers who have created something great, for example, those who have undertaken an enterprise or a country and have had great reputations. Instead of being proud of themselves, they still work with other people with a peaceful heart the same as those ordinary people.

Do you agree with me?

With much respect to the plum blossoms, I translated this poem and created a piece of music for them in 2006; then I created a painting for them in 2012, and painted two paintings to match this poem and the music as my assignment at Chinese National Academy of Arts in 2012.

Vocabulary

早梅　　zǎo méi　　the title of the poem meaning the plum blossoms in the early spring

早　　zǎo　*adv. / n.*　early

梅　　méi　*n.*　plum blossom, plum blossom tree

张谓　　zhāng wèi　　a poet's name in the Tang Dynasty

唐　　táng　*n.*　the Tang Dynasty (618 – 907)

一树寒梅白玉条　　yī shù hán méi bái yù tiáo　　Flowers cover a plum blossom tree like the white jade in the cold.

一　　yī　*numeral*　one, a

树　　shù　*n.*　tree

寒　　hán　*adj.*　cold

白玉　　bái yù　*n.*　white jade

白　　bái　*adj.*　white

玉　　yù　*n.*　jade

条　　tiáo　*n.*　bar, piece, here it means "branch"

迥临村路傍溪桥　　jiǒng lín cūn lù bàng xī qiáo　　Far away from the village road and near the bridge over the stream.

迥　　jiǒng　*adv. / adj.*　far away

临　　lín　*adv.*　near

村路　　cūn lù　*n.*　village road

村　　cūn　*n.*　village

路　　lù　*n.*　road, way

傍　　bàng　*adv.*　be close to, near

溪　　xī　*n.*　stream, brook

桥　　qiáo　*n.*　bridge

不知近水花先发　　bù zhī jìn shuǐ huā xiān fā　　I did not know the

flowers by the water would blossom earlier.

不　　bù　*adv.*　no, not

知　　zhī　*v.*　know, realize

近　　jìn　*adj.*　near

水　　shuǐ　*n.*　water, river, sea, stream

花　　huā　*n.*　flower, blossom

先　　xiān　*adv.*　first, earlier, at the first, here it means the earliest

发　　fā　*v.*　leave, set off, here it means "open", "blossom"

疑是经冬雪未消　yí shì jīng dōng xuě wèi xiāo　I thought it was the winter snow had not melted yet.

疑　　yí　*v.*　doubt, suspect, think

是　　shì　*v.*　be, is, are

经　　jīng　*v.*　pass, experience

冬　　dōng　*n.*　winter

雪　　xuě　*n.*　snow

未　　wèi　*adv.*　not

消　　xiāo　*v.*　melt, disappear

一树寒梅白玉条，迥临村路傍溪桥。不知近水花先发，疑是经冬雪未消。yī shù hán méi bái yù tiáo, jiǒng lín cūn lù bàng xī qiáo。bù zhī jìn shuǐ huā xiān fā, yí shì jīng dōng xuě wèi xiāo。

Flowers cover a plum blossom tree like the white jade in the cold,

Far away from the village road and near the bridge over the stream.

I did not know the flowers by the water would blossom earlier.

I thought it was the winter snow had not melted yet.

12. 竹石—Bamboos on the Rocks

竹 石—zhú shí

清—qīng 郑燮—zhèng xiè

咬定青山不放松—yǎo dìng qīng shān bù fàng sōng，
立根原在破岩中—lì gēn yuán zài pò yán zhōng。
千磨万击还坚劲—qiān mó wàn jī hái jiān jìn，
任尔东西南北风—rèn ěr dōng xī nán běi fēng。

Bamboos on the Rocks

By Zheng Xie   Qing Dynasty

Cling to the green mountain, never give up,
The bamboos take their roots in the cracks of the rocks.
Though they suffer, they are still strong,
Hold unyieldingly, no matter where the winds blow.

About the Poet

Zheng Xie 郑燮 zhèng xiè (1693 – 1765) was a famous poet, calligrapher and artist in the Qing Dynasty (1616 – 1911) and one of the Eight Eccentrics of Yangzhou (a group of eight painters in the Qing Dynasty) . He was from Xinghua of Jiangsu Province; his original family home is Suzhou.

Zheng's father was a teacher who taught hundreds of students. However, when Zheng Xie was born, his family was in restrained circumstances: his mother died when he was 3 or 4 years old and at the age of 14 his stepmother passed away.

Following his father, Zheng Xie started to read at the age of 3, wrote articles at 8 or 9 and wrote poems and lyrics when he was 16 years old.

He earned the title of Xiu Cai—a successful candidate in the imperial examination at the county level when he was 20; got the title of Ju Ren— a successful candidate in the imperial examinations at the provincial level at 40 years old and gained the title of Jin Shi—a successful candidate in the highest imperial examinations when he was 43 years old.

Despite this, he lived a poor life and he had to sell his paintings in Yangzhou so that he could support his family. Not until he was 50 years old was he appointed as a County Magistrate, first in Fan County and then in Wei County in Shandong Province. He was then fired from these positions, and he went back home to spend his time painting.

As an official, Zheng Xie loved his people as he loved his own sons. One year when he was the magistrate in Wei County there was a famine. Despite strong opposition from his superiors, he kept the granaries opening and saved more than ten thousand lives. With this kind of responsible attitude to his work, there were no cases of injustice during his tenure as County Magistrate. He was so much appreciated that the local people built a memorial temple for him. However, what he had done annoyed his superiors and he was fired so he went home to paint.

In 1748, when Emperor Qianlong inspected Shandong, he appointed Zheng Xie as the Shuhua Shi—official Historian of Calligraphy and Painting; he participated in the preparatory work for the emperor to climb the Tai Mountains.

At least 5 of his books are still extant.

As an artist, Zheng Xie's calligraphy, painting and poetry were called the Three Matchless skills.

In calligraphy, he combined the "草隶篆楷—Cao (cursive hand—characters executed swiftly and with strokes flowing together), Li (official script—an ancient style of calligraphy current in the Han Dynasty 206 B. C. – 220 A. D.), Zhuan (seal character—a style of Chinese calligraphy, often used on seals) and Kai (regular script)", together with his own orchid and bamboo painting style, the big or small size and the deflection style, to create his own style which he humorously called "六分半书— (liù fēn bàn shū)", meaning that it is made of four ancient calligraphy styles plus his own two and a half styles.

In painting, his favorite subjects were bamboo, orchid and stone, and he said he painted "四时不谢之兰，百节长青之竹，万古不败之石，千秋不变之人 sì shí bù xiè zhī lán, bǎi jié cháng qīng zhī zhú, wàn gǔ bù bài zhī shí, qiān qiū bù biàn zhī rén" —the orchid that does not wither in the four seasons; the bamboo with a hundred joints that is evergreen; the rock that does not crumble throughout the ages and people who are unchanged forever.

In poetry, most of his Ti Hua Shi—poems on the paintings, were made after he was fired. He said to himself "宦海归来两袖空，逢人画竹卖清风 huàn hǎi guī lái liǎng xiù kōng, féng rén huà zhú mài qīng fēng" —With two clean hands, I have come back from official circles; as soon as I meet people, I sell my bamboos with the clean wind to them. (两袖清风 liǎng xiù qīng fēng : keep two clean hands during the time he was an officer, meaning that an honest official is not corrupt and lives a simple life all the time.)

Zheng Xie's Ti Hua Shi—poems on the paintings, departed from the tradition of poems on paintings where either the poem is a subsidiary of the painting or the painting is a subsidiary of the poem. The content of his poems always relates to real life. Through painting of admiring the bamboo, orchid and stone he is admiring people who are firm and unyielding, upright and selfless, gritty, honest, noble and so on. Each line expresses some idea of the poet; there is a far-reaching artistic conception.

Writing a poem on a painting also helps to continue and enlarge the stillness of the moment of the picture, adding to the artistic influence of the painting.

Zheng Xie is really one of the creators of the Ti Hua Shi in Chinese poetry history.

Ti Hua Shi—Poem on Chinese Painting or Painting Poem

Ti Hua Shi usually refers to a poem on a Chinese painting. It is used to express the feelings, artistic opinion or artistic conception of the author. Just as Fang Xun in Qing Dynasty said："高情逸思，画之不足，题以发之 gāo qíng yì sī, huà zhī bù zú, tí yǐ fā zhī"—Noble feelings or surpassing thoughts cannot be fully expressed by a painting alone, a poem can extend them.

A poem in calligraphy inscribed on a painting together with a stamp is a special characteristic of Chinese art. It is a unique style of Chinese painting and is considered to be a unique aesthetic phenomenon in the world of art history. There are many excellent Ti Hua Shi and they are not only a valuable inheritance, but they are also important in the history of Chinese literature.

Before the Song Dynasty (960 – 1279), poems that were not written on paintings, but expressed the poet's feelings about some paintings could also be called Ti Hua Shi in the broad sense of the term.

There are two theories concerning the origin of Ti Hua Shi. One states that it started in the Wei (220 – 265), Jin (265 – 420), and Southern and Northern Dynasties (420 – 589), the other says it started in the Song Dynasty (960 – 1279).

Zheng Xie and the 7 others of the Eight Eccentrics of Yangzhou are acknowledged as the best creators of Ti Hua Shi in the history of Chinese painting and poetry.

Traditional "Ti Hua Shi" was written on the blank part of a painting to help give the painting balance. Zheng Xie and the 7 others of the Eight Eccentrics of Yangzhou's poems on their paintings developed it to a new phase.

As a representative of the Eight Eccentrics of Yangzhou, Zheng Xie not only wrote a poem on his every painting, but he also wrote his poems in a style combining calligraphy and painting together—using the four kinds of traditional Chinese calligraphy with his painting, poetry and calligraphy together. His calligraphy became a close part of his painting; his paintings were pictures and also poetry.

With the creative style of combining poetry, calligraphy, painting and stamp together perfectly, Zheng Xie and the 7 others of the Eight Eccentrics of Yangzhou extended the content of the traditional Flower and Bird Painting, made literati painting more accessible to ordinary people, created a wonderful comprehensive art, and had much more influence in their society and on later generations.

Enjoy the Poem

This is a Ti Hua Shi—poem on the painting and Yong Wu Shi—a poem that expresses people's aspirations, emotions through chanting (writing) about a thing / object, and was written to complement the artistic conception of his bamboo paintings.

Since the Song Dynasty, bamboo has been praised as one of the four gentlemen of the flowers—plum blossoms, orchid, bamboo and chrysanthemum. It is the symbol of the qualities of modesty, straightness, rectitude, nobleness, tenacity and doggedness; it does not bend no matter how harsh the wind is and never "goes with the flow".

The title: 竹石 zhú shí, Bamboos on the Rocks or the Bamboo on the Rock.

The first line: 咬定青山不放松 yǎo dìng qīng shān bù fàng sōng— Cling to the green mountain, never give up.

This line writes about the roots of the bamboos, how they take their roots into the green mountain, just like a person who "bites" something and never lets go. The words "咬定 yǎo dìng—bite /cling firmly", endow the bamboos a human quality; both the features and the character of the bamboos and the people who share its qualities stand vividly revealed on the paper.

The second line: 立根原在破岩中 lì gēn yuán zài pò yán zhōng— The bamboos take their roots in the cracks of the rocks.

This line explains why the bamboos can bite /cling firmly to the green mountain, because they have taken their roots deeply into the rocks. With the word "破 pò—break / crack of", the poet indicates the poor living condition of the bamboos.

Anyway, even though in the riprap, the bamboos still take their roots inside, just like the pine that Mr. Tao Zhu wrote: "不择地势，不畏严寒酷热，随处苗壮地生长起来 bù zé dì shì, bù wèi yán hán kù rè, suí chù zhuó zhuàng de shēng zhǎng qǐ lái" —it does not choose the topography, it does not fear deep cold or intense heat, and it grows healthily and strongly everywhere.

Since they can live in such a difficult environment, lacking both soil and water, the implication is that the bamboos would be able to withstand any tribulation. This line is a continuation of the previous line and an

81

introduction to the following line.

The following two lines explain that even though the bamboos have experienced much hardship in the rain, snow and thunderstorms and have been shaken violently by the wind, they still stand firm.

The third line: 千磨万击还坚劲 qiān mó wàn jī hái jiān jìn—Though they suffer, they are still strong.

It is an analogy with the cold hardening of metal by striking it many times with a hammer, the bamboos have become stronger, standing upright and firmly in the wind, never bending with the wind.

The last line: 任尔东西南北风 rèn ěr dōng xī nán běi fēng —Hold unyieldingly, no matter where the winds blow .

With the words "千磨万击 qiān mó wàn jī—go through much suffering", showing us how bad the environment is; with "东西南北风 —the four winds" indicating the bad forces and the characteristics of the times that the poet lived in and the environment that the bamboos live in, both the poet and the bamboo have been inosculated as a whole.

When I write here, I cannot help thinking of the other poem *Ting Zhu—Bamboo in the Courtyard* by Liu Yuxi. If in that poem the bamboo is like a gentleman, then in this poem, the bamboo is more like a fighter.

With the method of personification, the author not only makes us feel a kind, true and natural beauty, we are also naturally influenced by the character of bamboo and the author.

With a superb ability, Zheng Xie used the usual common verbs to produce a charming and wonderful artistic conception for the poem.

In four short lines, a clear picture has been shown to us: under the cliff, in the cracks of the rocks, several green bamboos proudly stand up in the wind, their roots clinging deeply in the cracks, they grow up strongly. Both their inner tenacity and straight outer shape are vividly revealed on the paper.

This poem purely writes about the bamboo in nature, but it is more of a sketch than an absolute copy. What is written and painted has a clear symbolic meaning.

On the surface, it writes about the bamboo, whereas, in fact, it writes about the poet himself. The abstract meaning is implied in the visual description and offers the reader double enjoyment.

Inspiration

This is one of my favorite poems. I love this poem because it speaks out what I am thinking in my mind and what I want to say in my heart. So, I see it as my motto, and I often use the lines in this poem to encourage myself to study, work and fight against sicknesses. It has been accompanying me in my study, thinking and exploration of the road to a comprehensive art since 2000; it has also been encouraging me to fight my sicknesses since 2009.

With so much respect to the bamboos in the poem and to the poet, I created a piece of music to go with this poem in 2011 and I painted two paintings as my assignments at Chinese National Academy of Arts to match them in 2012.

Vocabulary

竹石　zhú shí　the title of the poem which means bamboos on the rocks

竹　zhú　*n.*　bamboo

石　shí　*n.*　rock, stone

郑燮　zhèng xiè　a poet's name in the Qing Dynasty

清　qīng　the Qing Dynasty (1616 – 1911)

咬定青山不放松　yǎo dìng qīng shān bù fàng sōng　Cling to the green mountain, never give up.

咬定　yǎo dìng　*v.*　cling firmly

咬　yǎo　*v.*　bite, here it means "cling to"

定　dìng　*adv.*　firmly

青山　qīng shān　*n.*　green/blue mountain

青　qīng　*adj.*　green, blue

山　shān　*n.*　mountain, hill

不放松　bú fàng sōng　do not loosen up, do not give up, never give up

不　bù　*adv.*　no, not

放松　fàng sōng　*v.*　loosen

立根原在破岩中　lì gēn yuán zài pò yán zhōng　The bamboos take their roots in the cracks of the rocks.

立　lì　*v.*　stand up

根　gēn　*n.*　root

原　yuán　*adv.*　originally

在　zài　*adv.*　in, on, at

破　pò　*adj.*　broken, here means the crack of the rocks

岩　yán　*n.*　rock

中　zhōng　*adv.*　in, inside, within

千磨万击还坚劲　qiān mó wàn jī hái jiān jìn　Though they suffer, they are still strong.

千磨万击　qiān mó wàn jī　go through much suffering

千　qiān　*quantifier*　thousand

磨　mó　*v.*　burnish

万　wàn　*quantifier*　ten thousand

击　jī　*v.*　beat, hit, strike

还　hái　*v.*　still

坚劲　jiān jìn　*adj./adv.*　strong and resolute; strongly and resolutely

坚　jiān　*adj./adv.*　*adj.* firm, strong, resolute　*adv.* firmly, strongly, resolutely

劲　jìn　*adj.*　strong; powerful; sturdy

任尔东西南北风　　rèn ěr dōng xī nán běi fēng　　Hold unyieldingly, no matter where the winds blow.

任　rèn　*adv.*　no matter

尔　ěr　*pron.*　you

东　dōng　*n.*　east

西　xī　*n.*　west

南　nán　*n.*　south

北　běi　*n.*　north

风　fēng　*n.*　wind, breeze

咬定青山不放松，立根原在破岩中。千磨万击还坚劲，任尔东西南北风。yǎo dìng qīng shān bù fàng sōng, lì gēn yuán zài pò yán zhōng。qiān mó wàn jī hái jiān jìn, rèn ěr dōng xī nán běi fēng。

Cling to the green mountain, never give up,

The bamboos take their roots in the cracks of the rocks.

Though they suffer, they are still strong,

Hold unyieldingly, no matter where the winds blow.

Afterword: Shirley's Dream Seeking Journey

When I had basically finished the work on this product, I felt that I should say something more.

Many friends are surprised that I am busy and there are always many things for me to do even though I have been free from my stressful career life in the securities industry.

The answer is: I am a dreamer.

I was lucky enough that I had made almost all my dreams come true in my former career field. Right now I can continue my childhood's dream, which may become my new career that I am going to pursue for the rest of my life.

Anyway, without the good guidance, help and support from so many good organizations and individuals, I wouldn't be the person who I am today.

With a grateful heart, I would like to thank the organizations below:
Missouri State University, USA
Springfield Regional Arts Council, Missouri, USA
Springfield Area Chamber of Commerce, Missouri, USA
Art Department of Drury University, Missouri, USA
Humanities & Fine Art Department of Ozarks Technical Community College, MO, USA

City of Pikeville, Kentucky, USA
Eastern Kentucky Expo Center, USA

The Artisan Alliance of Pikeville City /Pike County, Kentucky, USA
Kentucky World Language Association, USA
Kentucky Chinese Teacher Association, USA
Confucius Institute at University of Kentucky, USA

Graduate School / Chinese Painting School at Chinese National Academy of Arts
Chinese Painting School at China Central Academy of Fine Arts
Jinan University Press

Beijing University Shenzhen Hospital
Shenzhen Far East Women and Children Hospital
Shenzhen Futian People Hospital
Shenzhen First, Second and Third People's Hospitals
Hospital of Shenzhen Armed Police Force

Shenzhen Securities Information Co. , Ltd.
Shenzhen Panorama Network Co. , Ltd.

Shenzhen E-Bridge Science and Technology Development Co. , Ltd.
Jiangsu E-Bridge Culture Development Co. , Ltd.

I would also like to thank: My Deceased Mother—My first Chinese language and music teacher.

My Father—My first art teacher.

My Deceased Elder Brother—A dear family member who has influenced me positively since my childhood.

My Son—My hope, happiness & motivation to live, work and study strongly, healthily and positively.

My Younger Brother & Sister in Law—Dear family members whom I can rely on at any time.

My Sister & Brother in Law—Dear family members whom I can count on always.

王立人先生 Mr. Liren Wang—My first professional art teacher, he opened my eyes by teaching me to pencil sketch, paint from nature, gouache and oils. He was the first to recognize my artistic potential when I was a teenager.

沈绍祖先生 Mr. Shaozu Shen—My boss after I graduated from university, he chose me as the first Chinese classical literature and language instructor at his college. The resulting 9 years of teaching experience laid a firm foundation for my present comprehensive art exploration.

王师勤博士与李肇文先生 Dr. Shiqin Wang and Mr. Zhaowen Li—My first bosses, tutors and guides in the Chinese securities consultation industry, the fruit of their teaching, which involved much effort on their part and the most strict training was a series of 6 books and that gave a strong professional foundation for me to enter the first Stock Exchange of PRC and to work in the Chinese securities field.

夏斌先生与武凤仪先生 Mr. Bin Xia and Mr. Fengyi Wu—My second bosses at the Shenzhen Stock Exchange and my first bosses in the Chinese securities news industry, the huge professional latitude and the enormous support that they gave me, aroused in me an endless positivity towards studying, creating and exploring. Not only did I become an expert in my field of work, giving rise to the brightest 10 years in my career, but also, the work on the Internet, newspaper, magazine, series books, database, CD, and multimedia products and management fields, laid the best basis for my present dream-seeking.

米盖尔·麦克维先生与约翰·海顿先生 Mr. Migual Mckelyel and Mr. John Hayden—My first American English teachers, with their good teaching and help, I translated my first books, containing at total of 0. 93 million words from English into Chinese and started my first cross-cultural study and work.

苏希嘉博士与陈洁平博士 Dr. Xijia Su and Dr. Jieping Chen—My first English consultants and proof-readers which they did for no cost, one studied and lived in America for 16 years and is now a Professor and Associate Dean at the China European International Business School; the other is a Canadian-Chinese and also a professor at the same school. I relied on their unselfish assistance and recommendation for my first cross-cultural publication to be published and become the foundation of my new publication.

查理·金先生 Mr. Charlie King—My deceased American art teacher, he led me to restart on the path of painting study and this has been a positive influence on me even to this day.

麦克·乔伊斯先生 Mr. Mike Joyce—My first English tutor from England. He checked and corrected all of my writing for this publication and has helped voluntarily for 8 years. Without his help, I would not have courage to start my web site and I would not have been able to complete this product.

马萱老师 Ms. Xuan Ma—My first music teacher, she taught me for 4 years and set me on the path of music writing and singing.

蒙伟业教授 Prof. Weiye Meng—My music writing director. He checked and corrected my music score, coached me in my singing, directed me in making the recordings and accompanied me on the piano for all the songs on the recording.

陶辉教授 Prof. Hui Tao—My first Chinese Flower and Bird Painting teacher, he taught me for 8 years and led me on the path of Chinese painting study.

郭亚凯老师 Mr. Yakai Guo—My first tutor at China Central Academy of Fine Arts, it was because of his good direction that I entered China Central Academy of Fine Arts, where I have been a full-time art student since 2010.

李刚老师 Mr. Gang Li—My first Chinese Landscape tutor at China Central Academy of Fine Arts, he taught me how to paint from a stone to a tree, and led me to the field of professional painting.

孙琪老师 Mr. Qi Sun—My first tutor at Chinese National Academy of Arts, he led me go to CNAA and find the best place to work on my dream.

饶晓斌 Mr. Robert Xiaobin Rao—My first tutor from Shenzhen Personnel Bureau and Shenzhen University. He recommended me to study abroad, then I got my first master degree and my art dream come true in USA.

克利夫顿·M. 斯玛特博士 Dr. Clifton M. Smart—The first President of an American University (Missouri State University) whom I wrote to. He read my letters in person and he asked his assistant to respond me quickly.

贝琳达·麦卡锡博士 Dr. Belinda McCarthy—The former Provost of Missouri State University. She approved my art exhibition in the university in 2010. It helped me have a temporary foothold while I waited for my work schedule to go to City of Pikeville, Kentucky in May, 2010. I then had an opportunity to see an American eye-doctor and the diagnosis on my eye problem in USA, was of much help in later diagnosis of my other sicknesses in China. Anyway, before she and her husband came to my art exhibition, I did not know her and did not even know there was a position called "Provost" in a university.

刘文豪博士 Dr. David Wenhao Liu—My first work partner and tutor from Stanford University and The University of California. If there was not the patient teaching over the long distance in phone calls for about 6 hours and the positive comments and judgment on my study ability at the most difficult time that I had prepared to give up studying abroad, I would not be able to get my master degree on the mainland of the United States.

大卫·梅纳特博士 Dr. David Meinert—My first professor in USA

and the Associate Dean of the College of Business at Missouri State University. His strict but humanized management style, gave me the confidence to complete my master degree even when I did not think that I could earn it.

安娜·布拉舍女士 Ms. Anna Brashers—My first "Guardian Angel" in USA, as the Administrative Assistant of the College of Business Administration at Missouri State University, she offered me the most help in my academic and personal life in the USA.

宫小欧先生 Mr. Xiaoou Gong—My first private tutor and schoolfellow in America, with his great effort and patience and in his vacation and free time, he helped me hold the essential knowledge and skills in the most difficult crosses. And then he found that I could paint and he introduced me to the local chamber of commerce and art organization.

布莱德·勃顿豪斯 Mr. Brad Bodenhausen—As my first sponsor, and the Executive Manager of Springfield Area Chamber of Commerce, Missouri, USA, he and his organization held my first art exhibition and my art dream became true in America in 2009.

丽雅·汉密尔顿女士 Ms. Leah Hamilton—As my first sponsor and the Executive Director of Springfield Regional Arts Council, Missouri, USA, she and her organization held my first art exhibition, my art dream realized again in America in 2009 and in 2010.

斯蒂芬妮·克拉姆女士 Ms. Stephanie Cramer—As my first art director in America, Director of Programs and Expositions of Springfield Regional Arts Council, Missouri, USA, she arranged every detail of my first art exhibition in USA.

兴华·海克女士与杰瑞·海克先生 Mrs. Hing Wah Hatch & Mr. Jerry Hatch—My first Taiwanese-American friend who is an art instructor and an American artist who is an assistant professor in Missouri State University, they offered the most help with my first cross-cultural and comprehensive art practice in USA.

罗宾·楼女士 Ms. Robin Lower—The Director of the Art and Design Gallery I knew at Missouri State University. She directed and helped me to hold my first art exhibition at MSU in 2010. She did almost everything to make the exhibition work.

托马斯·林博士 Dr. Thomas Lane—The first Director of Student Union I knew in USA. He and his assistant did every detail things and arranged everything, helped and supported me to ensure the exhibition worked at Missouri State University.

爱德华·张先生 Dr. Edward Zhang—The first and the only American-Chinese professor who taught me face to face at Missouri State University. He helped me by doing the most logistics jobs on my cross-cultural communications in USA in 2010.

秦惠萍博士与皮特·梅德林博士 Dr. Huiping Chinn & Dr. Peter Meidlinger—The first professors I knew at Drury University. They facilitated my first two Chinese painting demonstrations in their university. Dr. Chinn personally created the poster for the event.

杰勒德·杰西卡博士 Dr. Gerard Jessica—The first instructor I knew at Ozarks Technical Community College. She arranged everything for my workshops at her college and she personally created a poster for me in 2010.

凯瑟琳·L. 克莱门博士 Dr. Catherine L. Clemens—The Head of the Humanities and Fine Arts Department at Ozarks Technical Community College. She was the first one who approved me to have a good Chinese art workshop at her college in 2010.

哈里特·米尔斯女士 Mrs. Harriet Mears—My first "American Mother" and former art instructor of Art Department at Drury University. She offered me free accommodation and looked after me very considerately when I was in USA in 2010.

乔·詹金斯先生 Mr. Joe Jenkins—The first successful American entrepreneur I knew. Both of he and his wife offered me much actual support and help by looking after 64 of my paintings in USA in 2010.

桂正梅女士 Mrs. Pat Hickey—My first "Elder Sister" in USA. She made appointments with doctors for me, drove me to see doctors at the time she herself was still sick. She also offered emergency assistance when I was working in an art fest in 2010.

邱晓先生 Mr. Xiao Qiu—My first "Temporary Son" and schoolmate at Missouri State University. He is as young as my son who is in Australia, but he offered most considerate help when I held my art exhibition in USA in 2010.

Mr. John David Lawson—The first American friend I knew from a church in USA and a Professor at Springfield Institute of Religion. He offered the most help in my study of Christianity by arranging 4 missionaries to help me learn *Bible*.

Ms. Tracy A. Gardner-Snodgrass, Ms. Erin Hughes, Ms. Kanvnila Price, Mr. Dave Cowens, Ms. Cindy Bylander, Mr. Calvin L. Allen, Ms. Rosliand, Ms. Stephanie Lemons, Mr. Kevin Zimmerman and Mrs. Wanda Rudolph—They organized the last 18 successful art workshops for me in their schools in MO, USA in 2009 and in 2010.

周毅然先生 Mr. Yiran Zhou—The first American Chinese teacher who I knew in Kentucky, USA, he found that I was doing a very interesting and meaningful work and he introduced me to an art authority and the local Chinese Teacher's Association.

比尔·布什博士 Dr. Bill R. Booth—The first American art professor that I knew in America, he was not only the first one to check my art study works from a professional angle in 2009 (and is still directing me now), but, he also personally drove for 2 hours to the City of Pikeville and introduced me to the local government.

修华静博士 Dr. Mask Huajing Xiu—The first Director of a Confucius Institutes whom I knew at University of Kentucky, USA. With a good insight, she found something meaningful in my comprehensive art and she invited me to share my ideas and explorations with more Chinese language teachers and students in USA.

兰迪·巴锐特先生 Mr. Randy Barrette—The first President of a Language Association whom I knew in USA (Kentucky World Language Association), with a good insight, he invited me to share my ideas with the local Chinese teachers in 2011 Kentucky World Language Conference. It gave me the first opportunity to summarize my study, thinking and exploration on theory. It became the landmark for me to enlarge my comprehensive art exploration into language field and a bigger market.

王燕女士 Mrs. Yan Wang —The first Chairman of the Chinese Teacher Association whom I knew in USA. She and her colleagues 李珊珊女士, Mrs. Shanshan Li, 塔拉·艾萨克女士 Ms. Tara Isaace, 陈红女士 Mrs. Hong Chen, 雷切尔·洛斯女士 Ms. Rachel Losch, 雷雪莲女士 Ms. Xuelian Lei, organized 18 Chinese art demonstrations and workshops for me at their schools in Kentucky, USA, in September, 2011.

林敏先生 Mr. Min Lin—The first editor I knew from an English newspaper in China. He discovered my efforts to bring Chinese art and culture to the outside world. He supported and encouraged me to open a column on Chinese culture in an English language newspaper.

张全先生 Mr. Charlie Quan Zhang—My first work partner of this project, without his support on technology, this product would not work.

郑颂博士与周明先生 Dr. Song Zheng and Mr. Ming Zhou—My last bosses in the Chinese securities multimedia information industry. With broad mind and good insight, they offered strong support during the time I was in USA, when I was sick, and then when I went to Beijing. This enabled me to keep studying, thinking and exploring my art dream until now.

张秋娟教授 Prof. Qiujuan Zhang, 刘郁博士 Dr. Yu Liu, 宋阳医生 Dr. Yang Song, 袁志东医生 Dr. Zhidong Yuan, 林琦医生 Dr. Qi Lin, 刘

映霞医生 Dr. Yingxia Liu, 刘蓉医生 Dr. Rong Liu, 龚敏护士长 Min Gong—My doctors and head-nurse from 7 hospitals in Shenzhen. If it were not for them, I would not be able to stand and would not be able to pursue my current dreams.

张树良先生 Mr. Shuliang Zhang, 于延杰女士 Ms. Yanjie Yu, 邵春先生 Mr. Chun Shao, 吴德华先生与曹雪芬女士 Mr. Dehua Wu and Ms. Xuefen Cao—They have done most jobs to help me in Shenzhen and Beijing.

王华博士与徐义雄先生 Dr. Hua Wang and Mr. Yixiong Xu—My first publishers in the art field, as the former and the current Presidents of Jinan University Press. By their good direction and help, my dream-seeking can go forward.

史蒂芬 · H. 罗宾耐特先生 Mr. Stephen H. Robinette—My first American advisor. As the Assistant Vice President of Missouri State University, at almost every key point, it was him who gave me the simplest but clearest opinions and directions.

蒋亚平教授 Prof. Yaping Jiang—My first director in the Internet field, as the founder of *People's Daily Online*, he has been a good advisor and supporter in the process of my cross-cultural and comprehensive art dream exploration.

霍学文先生 Dr. Xuewen Huo—The first government officer I thought of at the moment that I thought I would pass away when some serious pains from several sicknesses hit me at the same time and I almost could not move because of the problem on my spine, I wished to get support from the Chinese government so that my little cross-cultural and comprehensive art exploration project could be continued. Even though we met just once 12 years ago, it was he who spent much time and energy encouraging, helping and directing me.

多诺万 · 布莱克波顿先生 Mr. Donovan Blackburn—The first sponsor of my art exhibition in Pikeville City, Kentucky, USA in 2013, as the city manager, he is one of the best supporters of my dream-seeking road.

斯蒂芬·St. 约翰先生 Mr. Steve St. John—An American friend who I haven't met and the General Manager of Eastern Kentucky Expo Centre, Kentucky, USA, where I was due to hold an art exhibition in 2010, When I called him to say that I had some health problems, he suggested that I gave up my visit to his city even though he had already started to promote the exhibition. He then liaised with local government to organize my art exhibition in Pikeville City in 2013.

丽·安·休斯女士 Ms. Leigh Ann Hughes—The Grant Administrator of City of Pikeville and the Director of the Artisan Alliance of Pikeville/Pike County. She and her team will be the sponsors of my new art exhibition and cross-cultural and comprehensive art practice in 2013, she has become one of the best supporters of my dream-seeking.

When I write here, I cannot help saying to myself, what a lucky person I am! If there wasn't so much good, helpful support from so many people and organizations, I would not be able to do anything, my dream could not come true at all.

With a grateful heart, I would really like to say: "Thank You, my good professors, teachers, bosses and friends, I will cherish my luck and do my best to work towards helping more people with what I have learned and created, while continuing to improve myself every day."

I am a dream-seeker forever...

Sincerely yours,

张一平 Shirley Yiping Zhang

May 4, 2013

I would like to dedicate this publication to
my family, doctors, tutors, bosses and
my friends, for their generous help,
guidance, support, care and love.

谨以此出版物献给我的家人、医生、导
师、上司与朋友，真诚感谢您的帮助、
指导、支持与关爱。

张一平
Shirley Yiping Zhang
May 4, 2013